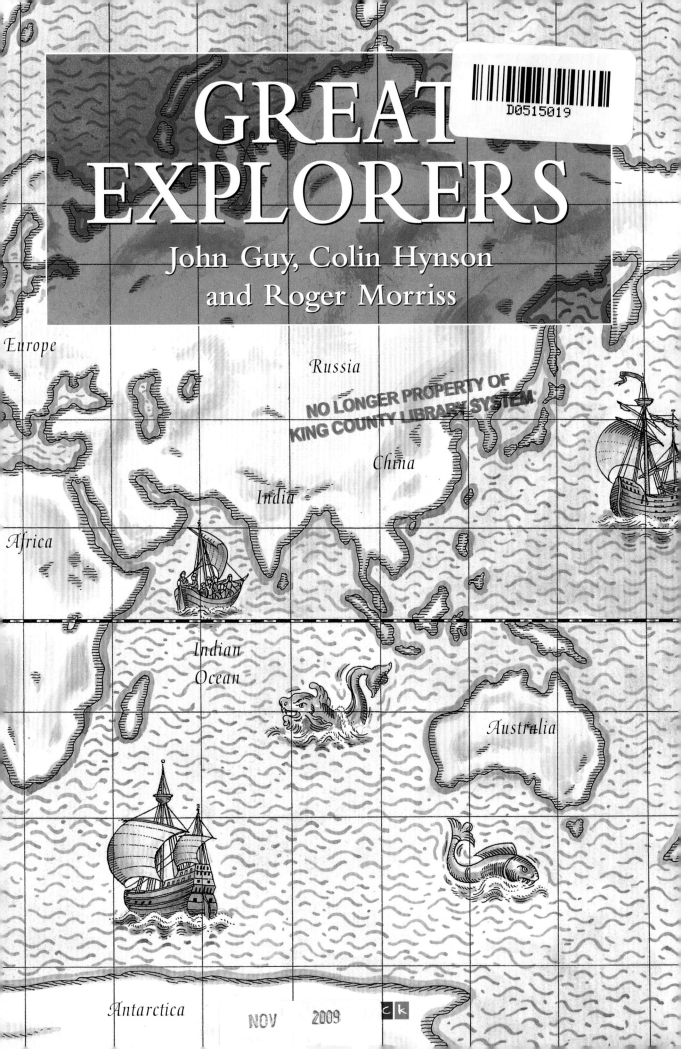

GREAT EXPLORERS

John Guy, Colin Hynson and Roger Morriss

Europe

Russia

China

India

Africa

Indian
Ocean

Australia

Antarctica

ACKNOWLEDGMENTS
Studio Manager: Sara Greasley
Editor: Claire Lucas
Production Controller: Ed Green
Production Manager: Suzy Kelly

We would like to thank: Graham Rich, Peter Done, John Guy, Val Garwood, and Elizabeth Wiggans for their assistance, and David Hobbs for his map of the world. Picture research by Image Sect.

North American edition copyright © ticktock Entertainment Ltd. 2010

First published in North America in 2010 by ticktock Media Ltd.,
The Old Sawmill, 103 Goods Station Road, Tunbridge Wells, Kent TN1 2DP, U.K.

ISBN: 978-1-84696-208-0 paperback

Printed in China
9 8 7 6 5 4 3 2 1

Picture credits (t=top; b=bottom; c=center; l=left; r=right; OFC=outside front cover; OBC=outside back cover):

AKG (London): 26br, 26–27t, 27tr, 27b, 27br, 28tl, 28bl, 29tl, 86c, 86–87cb, 87br, 94tl, 94–95c, 95cr, 96br, 96–97c, 97tr, 98tl, 98–99cb, 99tl, 100tl, 100–101c, 101tr, 118tl, 118bl, 119tr, 123. Ancient Art and Architecture: 90–91ct, 92bl, 118r, 119bl, 119br. Archivo Fotografico (Spain): 16tr, 22l, 103tr. Asia (Barcelona): 16cb, 17tr, 30cb, 30bl, 32cl, 89c, 94bl, 98bl, 99tr, 101br, 103br, 112tl. Bridgeman (London): 37tl, 37bl, 49cr, 80cb. Bridgeman/Giraudon (France): 108–109c, 109b. David Doubilet (National Geographic Society): 60–61. et Archive: 30tl, 90bl, 91tr, 95tr, 96c, 97br, 100bl, 121br. Chris Fairclough/Image Select: 20cb, 86–87c, 121tr. Fotomas Index: 16tl. Robert Garvey: 60–61b. Giraudon (France): 2–3ct, 4b, 14tl, 14–15, 15ct, 16c, 18–19ct, 23tr, 32–33ct, 32–33c, 84tr, 84c, 92t, 92–93c, 98–99c, 118c. Hannes Grobe (Creative Commons CC-BY-SA-2.5): 124. Ann Ronan/Image Select: 6bl, 10–11cb, 15tr, 19b, 21r, 23br, 26tl, 26–27c, 28br, 29tr, 31cr, 88bl, 89t 108tl, 121tl. Image Select: 7tr, 16–17cb, 19c, 29bl, 30–31c, 31br, 42bl, 89br, 90tl, 96tl, 98bl, 104l, 104b, 104–105c, 105br, 108tl, 115tr. Index (Spain): 32bl, 33br, 33c, 100–101bc, 102cl, 102–103c 120–121c. Index/Giraudon: 91br. Institut Amatller D'art Hispanic (Spain): 3, 20–21c, 22–23c, 103bl, 106tl. iStock: OFCt (background), OFCc, OFCbr, OBCt (background). John Lancaster: 60l. Antonia Macarthur: 60cb. Mary Evans Picture Library: 8tr, 8–9ct, 9tr, 10tl, 10bl, 11c, 18cl, 20–21cb, 37cr, 38t, 39br, 40c, 40tr, 40–41c, 40–41cb, 41br, 42–43cb, 43cb, 44t, 44bl, 46tr, 48tl, 48–49c, 49tr, 78bl, 80tl, 80tr, 80–81cb, 82–83cb, 83br, 84–85cb, 86bl, 87tl, 88tl, 88–89c, 102b, 112bl, 112–113cb, 113t, 113br, 114tl, 114bl, 115r, 116t, 116–117, 117tl. Mary Rose Trust: 6tl. NASA: 5b, 125. National Maritime Museum: 4–5c, 5t, 8tl, 8–9c, 9br, 8bl, 10–11ct, 11tr, 15br, 36br, 37bl, 39cl, 42cl, 44br, 45br, 46cr, 46–47, 47tr, 48bl, 49l, 49tr, 52–53 all, 54–55 all, 56l, 56cl, 56–57c, 57 all, 58–59 all, 62–63 all, 64tl, 64bl, 64–65b, 65br, 66–67 all, 68–69c, 68tl, 69tr, 70–71, 72–73, 74–75, 76l, 76t, 76c, 77 all, 78tl, 78–79cb, 79t, 80tl, 80c, 81br, 82l, 82–83c, 83t, 85br, 110-111 all, 112–113c, 114–115c, 122. By courtesy of the National Portrait Gallery, London: 76cb. The Natural History Museum, London: 64c, 65c. PIX: 20tl, 30tr, 32br, 38br, 43c, 108tr. Planet Earth Pictures: 106–107. Richard Polden: 60ct. Nick Saunders/Barbara Heller/Werner Forman Archive: 94bl, 102tl. Shutterstock: OFC (main background), OFCtl, OFCtr, OFCcr, OBC (main background), OBCtr, OBCtl, OBCbl. Spectrum Colour Library: 15tl, 18bl, 19tr, 105tr, 106–107ct, 109cr, 113tr. Trip/Darren Maybury: 22cb. Joe Tyrrell: 61br. Courtesy of The Ulster Museum (Belfast): 42–43ct. Werner Forman Archive: 84b, 86tl, 90br, 95br. West Devon Borough Council: 23bl. Cary Wolinsky (National Geographic Society): 65t, 69tl. Cary Wolinsky (The Natural History Museum, London): 56cb.

CONTENTS

Introduction

Exploration, the discovery of new lands, peoples, and cultures, has existed as long as humankind itself.

It was during the Age of Exploration between the 1400s–1600s that exploration and discovery became increasingly important. It was the need for power and trade, especially for spices and precious metals, that drove European explorers to seek out new trading partners and lands to colonize. Along with improvements in shipbuilding, map reading, and navigation, this was a time of great change in the European view of the world.

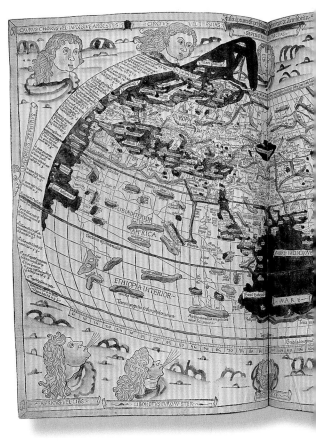

Since the time of the ancient Greeks, people had believed that Earth was at the center of the universe, with the Sun, Moon, and planets rotating around it. This was known as the Ptolemaic (or geocentric) model. This theory remained until the late 1500s, when it was replaced by the Copernican (or heliocentric) model, championed by Nicolaus Copernicus and later Galileo Galilei, in which the planets rotate around the Sun. The people of medieval Europe had a very different view from those today about the rest of the world. They did not have the benefit of newspapers, telephones, or television, so news hardly ever reached ordinary people. Unlike today, they were not able to fly from one continent to another. In fact, very few people went farther than their closest town during their whole lives. However, the way that medieval Europe looked at the world was to be changed forever by two explorers: Christopher Columbus, who sailed westward and found a new world in the Americas, and Vasco da Gama, who sailed eastward and found a sea route to Asia.

CHRISTOPHER COLUMBUS

Christopher Columbus's intention was to find a westward route to China and the East Indies, as an eastward route was blocked by Muslim lands hostile to Europeans. Although Columbus never found Asia during his voyages, he did discover the continent of South America after sailing across the Atlantic Ocean in 1492. He held the belief that it would be possible to continue sailing westward to reach Asia via South America.

FERDINAND MAGELLAN

Columbus's dream inspired Ferdinand Magellan, whose voyages proved that, as Columbus believed, it was possible to reach Asia by traveling westward. Magellan traveled around South America, and across the Pacific, discovering the Strait of Magellan.

FRANCIS DRAKE

Francis Drake became the first Englishman to successfully circumnavigate the globe. He was comissioned by Queen Elizabeth I to sail across the southern Atlantic through the Strait of Magellan and to attack the Spanish treasure ships and settlements on the unprotected west coast of South America.

A VIEW OF THE WORLD

This map was first produced in 1482 and is called Ptolemy's world map. It shows how little of the world Europeans really knew about. Southern Africa, the Pacific, and the North American continent are not included, and Asia seems to be a matter of guesswork. Only the mapping of the Mediterranean is accurate. Even the outlines of Scotland and Ireland look strange to modern eyes.

JAMES COOK

James Cook was a naval captain, explorer, and cartographer of world reknown. He made three voyages to the Pacific, becoming the first European to come into contact with the east coast of Australia, which he claimed for King George III and named New South Wales.

Despite the pioneering exploration of this time and the many journeys of later explorers over the years, there are still many places left for humankind to explore today; the depths of the ocean remain a mystery, as does the vastness of space. NASA, the National Aeronautics and Space Administration, was established in 1958 by President Dwight D. Eisenhower. One of the goals of NASA is to pioneer space exploration and, in the not too distant future, to send humans farther into space than they have ever been before.

THE KEPLER MISSION

On March 6, 2009, NASA successfully launched the Kepler Mission, a space telescope. It is designed to search our region of the Milky Way for Earth-size and smaller planets orbiting other stars that could be habitable and to discover how many of these planets there are in our galaxy.

Ships & Sailing

The crews of the early voyages of exploration faced many dangers. Not only did they have to put up with cramped conditions and a small supply of food and water (which was often bad), but they were also sailing into the unknown, with little idea where they were and how fast they were traveling. Perhaps it is not surprising that Christopher Columbus and others often faced mutiny. Today, ships have little trouble locating their exact positions. Accurate maps, clocks, and even Global Positioning Systems (GPS) mean that sailors can tell where they are to within a few feet. Sailors in the 1400s and 1500s were not so fortunate.

MAGNETIC COMPASS

It was very important that the sailors crossing the Atlantic knew the exact direction in which they were sailing. On a clear day or night, either the Sun or Polaris, the polestar, was used. They could also use a magnetic compass. The magnetic field around Earth meant that a magnetized needle floating in water would always point northward.

DEAD RECKONING

If a navigator knew from where his ship had sailed, its speed, the direction it was traveling, and how long they had been traveling, it was possible to calculate how far they had traveled by dead reckoning and thus find their position. However, winds and tides meant that this was only an approximate way of figuring out a ship's position. Columbus was regarded as a great navigator because of his skill with dead reckoning.

THE ASTROLABE

Every navigator in Columbus's time made use of the astrolabe (similar to this Arabic example). It could be used for finding out how far north or south of the equator (latitude) a ship was. It worked by measuring the height of the polestar or noon Sun from the ship. Once the height was known, the navigator could calculate how far north or south he was.

THE CROSS STAFF

The simplest way to measure the latitude of a ship was to use an instrument called a cross staff. It had a crossbar for sighting and a rod with measurements cut into the side. The crossbar would be lined up between the Sun or polestar and the horizon. The measurements of the long piece of wood would then tell the navigator the angle of the Sun or star from the horizon. From he could figure out the latitude. Bu is considerable danger in staring a the Sun for too long. In 1595, Captain John Davis invented the back staff, which used mirrors and shadows so that navigators did not risk being injured.

TELLING TIME

In order for a navigator to calculate a ship's position, it was vital that he knew what time of day it was. Sailors would be given the job of watching a large sand-filled hourglass (similar to this 17th-century example, shown here). It normally emptied after 30 minutes, and then a bell would be rung so that everybody onboard knew what time it was.

THE QUADRANT

Alongside the astrolabe, it is likely that Columbus used quadrants. When Ferdinand Magellan started on his famous voyage around the world in 1519, he brought seven astrolabes and 21 quadrants. Quadrants did the same job as astrolabes. They worked by lining up one arm with the horizon and then rotating a movable arm so that it was pointing at either the Sun or the polestar. The angle between these two arms could then be used to calculate the ship's latitude. It worked only when the sea was calm.

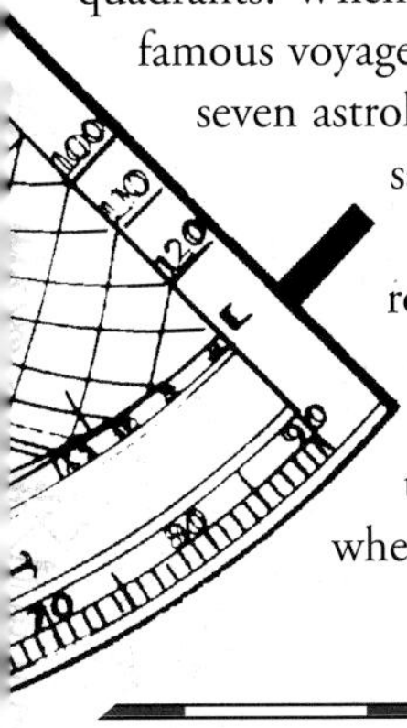

Navigation

In these days of radar, computer technology, and satellites, it is easy to underestimate the great navigational skills of the Elizabethan seafarers. For the most part they were sailing uncharted waters and had to estimate their locations as best they could, using only the positions of heavenly bodies to guide them. Until the development of more refined instruments, such as the chronometer in the mid-1700s, navigation was a very inexact science and relied heavily on the observational skills of the individual. Needless to say, there were many accidents, especially if ships were blown off course by bad weather into unknown waters.

GUIDED BY THE STARS

During the 1500s, the cross staff became commonly used to calculate a ship's latitude (north–south position) at night. It comprised two pieces of wood, similar in appearance to a crossbow, with graduated scales marked along the length. By observing the angle between the horizon and Polaris (the polestar or North Star) and taking a reading from the scales, coupled with a compass reading, the ship's approximate position could be calculated. Shown here is a buck staff, invented in around 1594, used for measuring the height of the Sun for the same purpose.

THE MARINER'S MIRROUR

Following Magellan's, and later Drake's, circumnavigation of the world, it became possible to more accurately assess Earth's size, which led to the production of more precise charts. The first sea atlas to be published in England, in 1588, was the *Mariner's Mirrour*. It was a collection of maps and charts showing the known coastlines of the world, derived from Dutch originals. The Dutch were an English ally against Spain and at the forefront of navigational techniques.

LODESTONE

One of the main problems facing Elizabethan navigators was accurately calculating a ship's longitude (east–west position). Here, astronomer-mathematician Flavius tries to do so by floating a piece of lodestone (a form of iron oxide) in a bowl of water while making calculations.

STEERING BY THE SUN

This view shows an Elizabethan navigator trying to calculate the ship's latitude by use of a compass and an early form of quadrant to measure the angle of the Sun's rays. However, precise timekeeping was necessary to ensure the accuracy of the calculations, so at best a ship's position could be only approximated. The first fully successful sea clock (chronometer) was not developed until 1759.

DRAKE'S DIAL

By Elizabethan times, compasses and other astronomical instruments had become sophisticated, as can be seen in this beautifully crafted astronomical compendium. It was made of brass in 1569 by Humphrey Cole, one of the finest scientific instrument makers of the time, and was once believed to have belonged to Drake himself. The compendium comprised a compass, along with lunar and solar dials that, as well as being astronomical aids, enabled the user to calculate the time. Engraved on the casing were the latitudes of many important ports around the world.

NAVIGATION
-A TIMELINE-

~1675~
Charles II founds the Royal Observatory in Greenwich, England.

~1714~
Board of Longitude is established to promote solutions for finding longitude at sea.

~1729~
John Harrison starts building his first experimental chronometer.

~1761~
Harrison's fourth chronometer (H4) is successfully trialed.

GETTING YOUR BEARINGS

The ancient Chinese discovered that lodestone is naturally magnetic and, if suspended on a string, will always point north. Early navigators made good use of this natural material, but it was somewhat crude. Sometime in the 1100s, European navigators discovered that a needle could be similarly magnetized by stroking it with lodestone. This discovery eventually led to the development of more sophisticated and accurate compasses, with the needle balanced on a central pivot. The example shown here is encased in an ivory bowl and dates from around 1580.

Life Onboard an Elizabethan ship

Life onboard ships in Elizabethan times was extremely harsh, and the pay (which was frequently overdue) was poor. But, faced with abject poverty at a time when many country people were being forcibly ejected from their land because of changing farming practices, many men had few options. A large proportion of a ship's crew would also have been criminals escaping the law, which often led to problems with discipline. The mortality rate among an average crew was very high, and it would be considered normal for a ship to return to port with only one fourth of the men alive. To ensure that they had enough men left to make the return trip, most captains oversubscribed when signing on a new crew, but this in itself led to problems of overcrowding and food rationing. Conditions onboard were cramped, with each man usually sleeping in a hammock slung below deck, and toilet facilities were virtually nonexistent.

JACK-OF-ALL-TRADES

A crew on an Elizabethan ship had to be completely self-sufficient, as they were often away at sea for several years and might go many months between landings. As well as being able to handle the ship, sailors had to master other essential skills such as carpentry, sail making, rope making, and cooking.

DRUNKENNESS

One of the most common problems facing any captain commanding an Elizabethan ship on a long voyage was boredom and the unruly behavior of his crew. With fresh water in short supply, the only drink available was beer (one gallon per crew member per day) or other stronger alcohol, which frequently led to drunkenness, not only onboard but also in port. Discipline was necessarily very harsh to avoid potentially fatal accidents at sea.

DISEASE

The most common disease encountered aboard a ship was scurvy, a deficiency of vitamin C, caused by lack of fresh fruit and vegetables. The symptoms include bleeding gums and loose teeth. Resistance to infection is also lowered, often resulting in death if untreated. All ships carried their share of rats, which might spread infectious diseases such as the plague. Other common diseases were malaria, typhoid fever, and dysentery.

THE CHATHAM CHEST

After the Spanish Armada assault of 1588, so many seamen were wounded and maimed that Sir John Hawkins and Sir Francis Drake established the Chatham Chest—the first seamen's charity. All sailors in the navy had to pay sixpence a month from their salary into it for welfare purposes. This is the chest of 1625.

THE ART OF THE GUNNER

Most Elizabethan ships carried a number of cannon (a mortar is shown here), usually made from cast iron or bronze. They were mounted on carriages and secured in place by heavy ropes to control the recoil when being fired and to prevent them from coming adrift in rough seas. They were used mostly to disable a ship before boarding.

HEALTH & SAFETY

The health and safety of the crew aboard a typical Elizabethan ship was, to say the least, extremely hazardous. There were many accidents in simply carrying out the day-to-day tasks of sailing. Injuries sustained during encounters with enemy vessels, usually at close quarters, were horrific. Most ships carried a surgeon, but the treatment he was able to administer was both limited and very crude. By far the most common form of treatment was the amputation of badly damaged or infected limbs. There was no anesthetic (other than to make the patient drunk), and the survival rate was very low. Many of those who survived surgery died from gangrene afterward.

DAILY SUSTENANCE

All the ship's food was prepared in the galley and then distributed among the crew. Food was rarely fresh and might consist of biscuits, salted beef, or fish, supplemented by cheese and gruel, a type of thin, watery porridge. Drinking water was usually scarce, but most ships carried a plentiful supply of beer. The pieces of tableware shown here were retrieved from Henry VIII's ship the *Mary Rose* and are typical of items in use throughout the Tudor period.

LIFE ONBOARD
-A TIMELINE-

~1558~
The Spanish Armada sails against England with the intention of overthrowing Queen Elizabeth I. The Armada is defeated.

~1590~
Sir John Hawkins and Sir Francis Drake found the Chatham Chest to support injured and disabled sailors.

~1594~
Sir John Hawkins founds the Hawkins Hospital in Chatham, England.

Greenland

Atlantic
Ocean

North
America

South
America

KEY

1st Voyage
2nd Voyage
3rd Voyage
4th Voyage

COLUMBUS

Europe

Russia

China

India

Africa

Indian
Ocean

Australia

Antarctica

This map shows the voyages
of Christopher Columbus.

Christopher Columbus

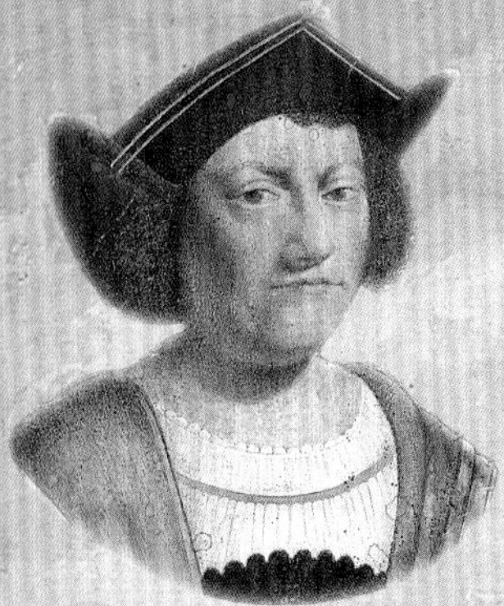

CHRISTOPHER COLUMBUS

Columbus was born into a family of weavers in Genoa, Italy, in around 1451. He had little education and could not read and write until he was an adult. Like many boys from Genoa, he became a sailor. In 1476, at the age of 25, he was shipwrecked off the coast of Portugal.

The main picture shows Christopher Columbus about to set off in 1492 on his historic voyage from Palos in Spain. His goal was not to discover a new land but to find a different passage to lands that were already known. He was seeking a westward route to China and India. It was almost impossible for Europeans to reach Asia by land, due to hostile Muslim lands in the east. Columbus was trying to find a way around this barrier.

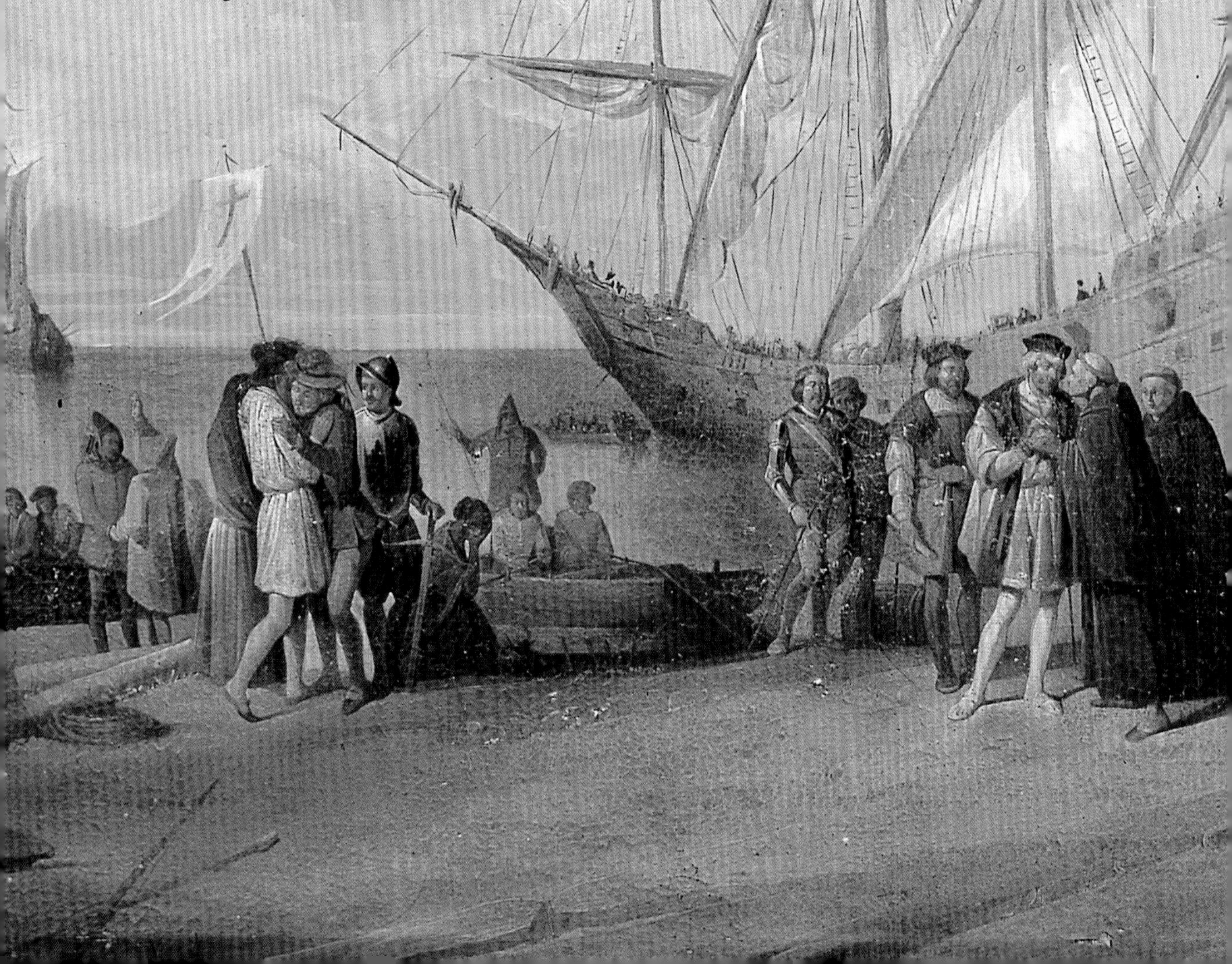

EXPERIENCE IN SAILING

After his shipwreck, Columbus stayed on in Portugal and settled in Lisbon. He got married, became a mapmaker, and continued his career as a sailor. He visited the West African coast, England, and Ireland. He later claimed that he had also sailed to Iceland.

THE WEALTH OF THE INDIES

Columbus called his plan "the enterprise of the Indies." When medieval Europeans used the word *Indies*, they did not mean just India but also Japan, China, Indonesia, and Southeast Asia. It was believed that these were all very wealthy lands. Using Marco Polo's calculations, Columbus figured out that India was around 3,900 mi. (6,300km) west of Europe. In fact, this is the approximate distance between Europe and the North American coast.

KING JOHN II OF PORTUGAL

It was while he was sailing in the Atlantic that Columbus deduced that it might be possible to sail westward from Europe to Asia. He first asked King John II of Portugal for help in 1484, but he was refused. The Portuguese were looking for a route to Asia around the African coast.

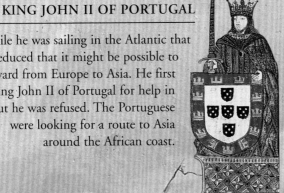

THE SPANISH INQUISITION

The Inquisition punished anyone who strayed from Roman Catholic teachings. They used torture to obtain confessions, and the guilty were often burned alive. In Spain, the Inquisition was used mostly against Jews, who were forced to convert to Christianity. Jews who refused to convert were ordered out of Spain on August 3, 1492, the day Columbus began his voyage across the Atlantic.

CHRISTOPHER COLUMBUS
-A TIMELINE-

~c. 1451~

Christopher Columbus is born in Genoa, Italy.

~1476~

Columbus is shipwrecked off Portugal and starts to work for the Portuguese.

~1484~

King John II of Portugal turns down Columbus's request for help to sail west.

~1485~

Columbus moves to Spain to look for help from King Ferdinand and Queen Isabella.

~1490~

The commission under Hernando de Talavera recommends that the Spanish royal family turn down Columbus's proposals.

HERNANDO DE TALAVERA

The king and queen of Spain set up a special commission of priests, astrologers, and scholars to look at Columbus's proposals. It was headed by Hernando de Talavera, who was a monk and Queen Isabella's confessor. This church (right) was named after him. The commission took until 1490 to come to a conclusion, and they advised the monarchs to reject Columbus's plan.

FERDINAND AND ISABELLA

Spain was divided into several kingdoms, the two largest being Castile and Aragon. The heir to the throne of Castile, Isabella, married the heir to the throne of Aragon, Ferdinand. When they both became the monarchs of their country, the two thrones ruled together. A unified Spain under Isabella I and Ferdinand II was now much stronger.

SANTÁNGEL THE TREASURER

Columbus needed friends at the royal court to put his case to the king and queen. One of his major supporters was Luis de Santángel, the treasurer, who looked after the finances of the two monarchs. Without his support, Columbus's plan would have been rejected.

The Court of Ferdinand & Isabella

The refusal of King John II of Portugal to fund Columbus's plan to sail across the Atlantic Ocean to the Indies must have been a terrible blow to him. One year after John II had turned him down, Columbus decided to move with his family to Spain to see if he could get support for his voyage there. A great deal of rivalry existed between Spain and Portugal, especially over finding a sea route to Asia. Columbus hoped to use this rivalry to convince the Spanish to support him and so have the advantage over the Portuguese. However, Columbus's plan to find a westward route to Asia seemed incredible to many people. Ferdinand and Isabella had to be convinced to finance a very risky venture.

THE NEED FOR GOLD

It was Ferdinand and Isabella's constant need for gold, even more than spices or silks, that made them finally accept Columbus's plan. The costs of waging war against the Moors and the expense of their magnificent court meant that they were very short of money.

THE *RECONQUISTA*

In the 700s, most of Spain was conquered by the Moors, Muslims from North Africa. The Spanish dreamed of driving them out and making Spain a Christian country again. Under Ferdinand and Isabella, the *Reconquista* (Reconquest) began, and by 1492, the Moors were finally pushed out of Spain, 700 years after they had first arrived.

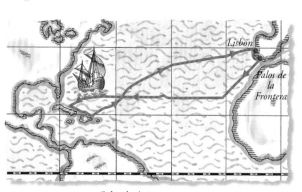

Columbus's 1st voyage ——

Columbus's First Voyage

t took another two years for Ferdinand and Isabella to accept Talavera's recommendations and turn down Columbus's proposals. He was extremely disappointed. He was contemplating approaching the king of France when he met a new ally, a ship owner named Martín Alonso Pinzón. Columbus returned with his new partner and again asked for royal support. He also demanded that he be made governor of any new lands he found and granted ten percent of all the gold, jewels, and spices. Ferdinand and Isabella refused him at first, but he gradually won them over. When he finally received royal approval, Columbus moved quickly. He and Pinzón soon had three ships ready to sail, and the trip began at dawn on August 3, 1492.

LAND SIGHTED AT LAST

After several false alarms, land was finally sighted by a member of Columbus's crew on October 12, 1492, more than two months after they had set off from Spain. The land found was one of the islands of the modern Bahamas. Columbus named it San Salvador. The local population was called the Arawak, but Columbus was convinced that he had arrived at the Indies, so he called them Indians.

DEALING WITH MUTINY

Once the ships were out of sight of land, many of the sailors became nervous. They knew that they would eventually reach land, but they were afraid that they might run out of food before then and could not return to Spain. Columbus prevented the crew from mutinying and forcing the ships to return to Spain by lying to them about how close they were to land.

SIGHTING OF A VOLCANO

After setting off from Spain, the ships landed at the Canary Islands to take on new supplies. While Columbus was there, a live volcano near Tenerife erupted on August 24, 1492. According to Columbus's journal, many of the crew, who were already nervous about the voyage, were frightened by the eruption. Columbus tried to explain what volcanoes were to the Spanish sailors.

THE SHIPS ON THE VOYAGE

Columbus took three ships on his trip across the Atlantic. They were the *Niña* (captained by Pinzón and his brother), the *Pinta*, and Columbus's own ship, the *Santa Maria*. The *Santa Maria* was just over 100 ft. long (around 30m), with the others at one half that length. The total crew for these three ships numbered 90 men.

RETURN TO SPAIN

When Columbus departed Hispaniola, he left behind 38 men and enough food and ammunition for one year. He and his crew moved onto the *Niña* and set off for Spain on January 4, 1493. The *Pinta* joined the *Niña* on January 6. Eventually, Columbus arrived at the Azores on February 18 and Portugal on March 4. Columbus then sailed to Palos, Spain, on March 15 and went to meet the king and queen in Barcelona in triumph.

CUBA AND ONWARD

After leaving San Salvador, Columbus arrived in Cuba. He was convinced that he had arrived in China and sent a team to find the "Great Khan." They came back after finding nothing. The ships then sailed to Haiti, which Columbus named Hispaniola (the "Spanish Island"). According to the first published account of the New World, in 1497, the people there lived to the age 150, had no government, and ate human flesh.

A NEW CONTINENT

During Columbus's later voyages, it became clear that he had not found a new route to the Indies. Instead, he had discovered a continent unknown to the Europeans. After meeting natives in Venezuela on his third journey in 1498, he wrote in his journal that he had found "a very great continent . . . where Christianity will have so much enjoyment and our faith in time so great an increase."

SHIPS FOR LATER VOYAGES

While Columbus had only three ships on his first voyage, things were very different for his second. Ferdinand and Isabella were so eager that Spain should stay in control of what they thought was the westward route to Asia that they gave Columbus 17 ships. The fact that his third voyage had only six ships and his fourth voyage just four shows how much Columbus fell from favor with Ferdinand and Isabella.

CHRISTOPHER COLUMBUS
-A TIMELINE-

~1492~
Columbus sets off on his first voyage and lands in San Salvador (Bahamas).

~1493~
Columbus returns to Spain and sets off on his second voyage.

~1498~
Columbus begins his third voyage.

~1500~
Columbus is arrested and sent back to Spain.

~1502~
Columbus sets off on his fourth and final voyage.

~1506~
Columbus dies in Valladolid, Spain.

THE DISCOVERY OF VENEZUELA

Columbus set of on his third voyage on May 30, 1498. He was searching for the mainland that he believed should have been close to the islands that he had discovered. After discovering the island of Trinidad in July 1498, he sailed to the coast of South America. On August 5, 1498, he landed on the coast of Venezuela and became the first European to set foot in South America. He also sighted the Orinoco River, which runs between Venezuela and Brazil. Columbus believed that Venezuela was part of an island and that Cuba was part of the mainland.

Columbus's Later Voyages

When Columbus arrived at the royal court in Barcelona, he was received by Ferdinand and Isabella with a great deal of honor.

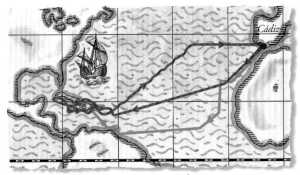

Columbus's 2nd voyage ——— 3rd voyage ———

Columbus had brought back some gold, amber, and an escort of Native peoples. Both monarchs were convinced that Columbus had reached the Indies. He was made governor of the Indies and "Admiral of the Ocean Sea." He was urged to start another expedition as soon as possible to explore and colonize the new lands. Ferdinand and Isabella were concerned that the Portuguese would send their own ships and claim the land as theirs, so Columbus went on another three voyages across the Atlantic, but none of them was as successful as the first.

COLUMBUS AS GOVERNOR

On his second voyage, Columbus returned to Hispaniola and found that the whole camp had been destroyed and the Spaniards killed. He ordered that a new colony called Isabela be built. In April 1494, he left to explore Cuba and Jamaica and returned to Isabela five months later as governor of the Indies. He was not a good leader. He argued with the Spanish nobles and administrators sent by Ferdinand and Isabella. He returned to Spain in June 1496 with none of the riches that he had promised the two monarchs.

SHIPWRECKED ON JAMAICA

Columbus's fourth and last voyage in 1502 was perhaps his most difficult. He had to pay for the trip himself. After dealing with a mutiny from his crew, a storm almost destroyed his ships, and he was shipwrecked on Jamaica for one year.

Columbus's Later Voyages

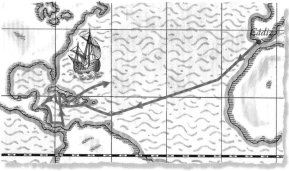

Columbus's 4th voyage ━━

Columbus fell gradually from favour at the Spanish court as his subsequent voyages proved less fruitful than the first. The king and queen remained loyal to him, but they realized that, while he was a great explorer, he was not competent as a governor. During his third voyage in 1498, he found that the colonists left behind from a previous trip were fighting among themselves. The two monarchs sent Francisco de Bobadilla to take over the governorship from Columbus. Columbus regarded this decision as a betrayal. He was arrested and sent back to Spain in 1500. Upon his arrival at court, Ferdinand and Isabella ordered his release. He was treated with respect, but they refused to make him governor of the "Indies" again. The French and English were beginning to explore the New World, and Spain needed someone capable to protect their interests there.

THE NEED FOR GOLD

The lack of gold brought back from Columbus's expeditions proved to be his downfall. He failed to convince his royal supporters that he had discovered a new route to Asia. His later voyages were also marred by ill-disciplined and gold-hungry crews.

VISITING THE MAINLAND

Columbus rarely visited the mainland of the South American continent. It was only on his third voyage that he eventually landed in Venezuela. On his fourth voyage, he explored the coast of Central America. He also visited the Gulf of Mexico and the coasts of Honduras, Nicaragua, Costa Rica (shown here), and Panama. He was still looking for a sea route to the Indies.

THE DEATH OF COLUMBUS

Columbus returned to Spain after his fourth and final voyage in November 1504. By this time, he was very sick and had to be carried to Seville. After Queen Isabella died, he was taken to see Ferdinand. Columbus said that he should be given back the governorship of the Indies. After Ferdinand refused, Columbus's health got worse. He wrote his will on May 19, 1506 and died the next day in Valladolid, Spain, a disappointed man abandoned by his monarchs

COLUMBUS'S SHIPS

On all his voyages, Columbus depended on a particular type of ship called a caravel. These ships normally weighed around 55 tons and had a crew of around 20. They had two masts. Their triangular sails made them easy to maneuver, and because they were not as heavy as other ships, they could be used in shallow water and along coastlines. This made them ideal for exploration. However, their small size was also a disadvantage. It meant that they could carry only limited amounts of food, water, and other supplies. On long voyages, an ever-present problem involved the ability to carry sufficient food and water for the duration of the trip. Gradually explorers began to use larger vessels called carracks to carry their provisions.

DIEGO COLÓN

Several members of the Columbus family took part in the early voyages. Columbus's brother, Bartholomew, was in charge of the colony of Isabela during his second voyage. Columbus's eldest son, Diego (on the left of the picture), served as a page to Prince Juan, the heir to the two thrones of Spain. When Columbus died, Diego was named admiral of the Indies and governor of Hispaniola. He continued to claim all the privileges that Ferdinand and Isabella first gave to his father. He was not successful.

Greenland

North
America

Atlantic
Ocean

N

South
America

KEY

—— *Ferdinand Magellan*

MAGELLAN

Europe

Russia

China

India

Africa

Indian
Ocean

Australia

Antarctica

This map shows the voyage of
Ferdinand Magellan.

Ferdinand Magellan

A WOODCUT PRINT
OF MAGELLAN

A WOODCUT PRINT OF MAGELLAN

Magellan was born in 1480 into a noble family in the Portuguese town of Sabrosa. He spent his early years as a page at the Portuguese royal court in Lisbon before joining the Portuguese navy.

When Christopher Columbus sailed across the Atlantic Ocean in 1492, his intention was to discover a westward route to China and the East Indies. An eastward route was blocked to Europeans by hostile Muslim lands. Columbus never found Asia, but he did discover, after four voyages, a continent virtually unknown to Europeans—South America. However, Columbus and others continued to believe that it was possible to journey westward and reach Asia by sailing around the South American continent. It was this dream that inspired Ferdinand Magellan to sail on a quest that would become the first voyage to circumnavigate the world. Magellan proved that it was possible to reach Asia by traveling to the west, but he paid for this discovery with his life—he was killed before the voyage was completed.

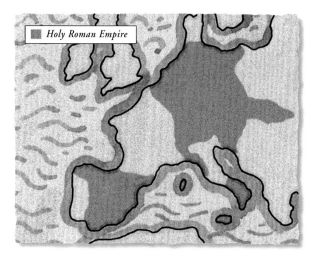

Holy Roman Empire

THE MOST POWERFUL MONARCH IN EUROPE

Charles V ruled over Spain, the Netherlands, southern Italy, most of modern-day Germany and Austria, and Spanish-conquered South America and Africa—the Holy Roman Empire. He provided the finances for Magellan's trip and continued to pay for the conquest and colonization of South and Central America.

THE TREATY OF TORDESILLAS

To prevent further rivalry between Spain and Portugal, Pope Alexander VI issued the Treaty of Tordesillas in 1494. This gave Spain control over all non-Christian lands west of an imaginary line in the mid-Atlantic. Portugal was given everything to the east.

THE RISE OF PORTUGAL

This engraving of Lisbon in the 1550s shows that Portugal was an important and wealthy seafaring and trading nation. Portugal had successfully freed itself from Muslim rule by 1250 and turned its attention to the exploration of the Atlantic coast of West Africa. The Portuguese discovery of a route around Africa to Asia meant that they controlled the spice trade to Europe. It was for this reason that Spain financed Magellan's trip to find an alternate route to the East.

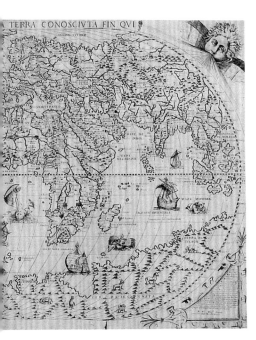

MAGELLAN TAKES TO THE SEA

While Magellan served with the Portuguese navy, he traveled to many parts of the world, including India and West Africa. He took part in battles against the Arabs on the Indian Ocean. Afterward he fought against the Moors in North Africa, where he was injured. He asked the king of Portugal, Manuel I, for an increase in his pension. Manuel replied by dismissing him, and Magellan offered his services to Charles V.

FERDINAND MAGELLAN
- A TIMELINE -

~1480~
Ferdinand Magellan is born.

~1505~
Magellan joins the Portuguese navy.

~1506~
Magellan sails to the East Indies.

~1513~
Magellan is injured while fighting in North Africa.

~1518~
After an argument with King Manuel I of Portugal, Magellan begins to work for Charles I who agrees to fund Magellan's voyage to find Asia.

KING JOHN II OF PORTUGAL

John II ruled Portugal from 1481 to 1495. He had been placed in charge of Portuguese explorations by his father in 1474, and he encouraged the exploration of the African coast and the Middle East. Columbus had asked him for money to finance his trip across the Atlantic, but John turned him down. In 1492, he admitted thousands of wealthy Jews into Portugal after they had been expelled by Spain, only to expel them a few years later in 1497–1498.

Preparing for the Voyage

I t took only two months for Magellan to convince Spanish King Charles I (he became Holy Roman Emperor Charles V in 1519) to finance his voyage to discover a westward route to Asia from the west. Charles I allowed Magellan to be commander of the fleet and to keep five percent of any profits made from the trip. Magellan took a close interest in how his ships were equipped, and records still exist that show exactly what Magellan took on his voyage. These include details of weapons, navigational instruments, food, and goods for trade. He had five ships: the *San Antonio*, the *Trinidad*, the *Concepción*, the *Santiago*, and the *Victoria*. The crews totaled over 230 and were of many different nationalities, including French, Portuguese, Italian, African, and Malaysian. Magellan was the only non-Spanish officer.

MAGELLAN'S SHIPS

Of the five ships in Magellan's fleet, four, including the *Victoria,* pictured here, were carracks. Carracks were large vessels that were originally built to be merchant ships. On expeditions they carried supplies and most of the weapons. The *Santiago* was a caravel. Caravels were much smaller and lighter, with triangular sails that made them better for navigating in coastal waters. Carracks had three masts or more, while a typical caravel had only two.

THE SUPPORT OF THE KING

Charles I approved Magellan's plan and agreed to pay for the voyage in September 1518. It took Magellan one year to gather together a crew and prepare his ships at the Spanish port of Sanlúcar in Seville. It is likely that Magellan had no intention of sailing around the world and was planning to return by the same route that he was to take from Spain.

A HUNTING FALCON

Magellan knew that if his trip was to be successful, he had to trade with people he met on his voyage. He took many things to barter with such as printed handkerchiefs, scissors, knives, glass beads, and around 20,000 bells that could be attached to the feet of trained hunting birds. European explorers had found that many people in both the Americas and Africa found hawk bells fascinating.

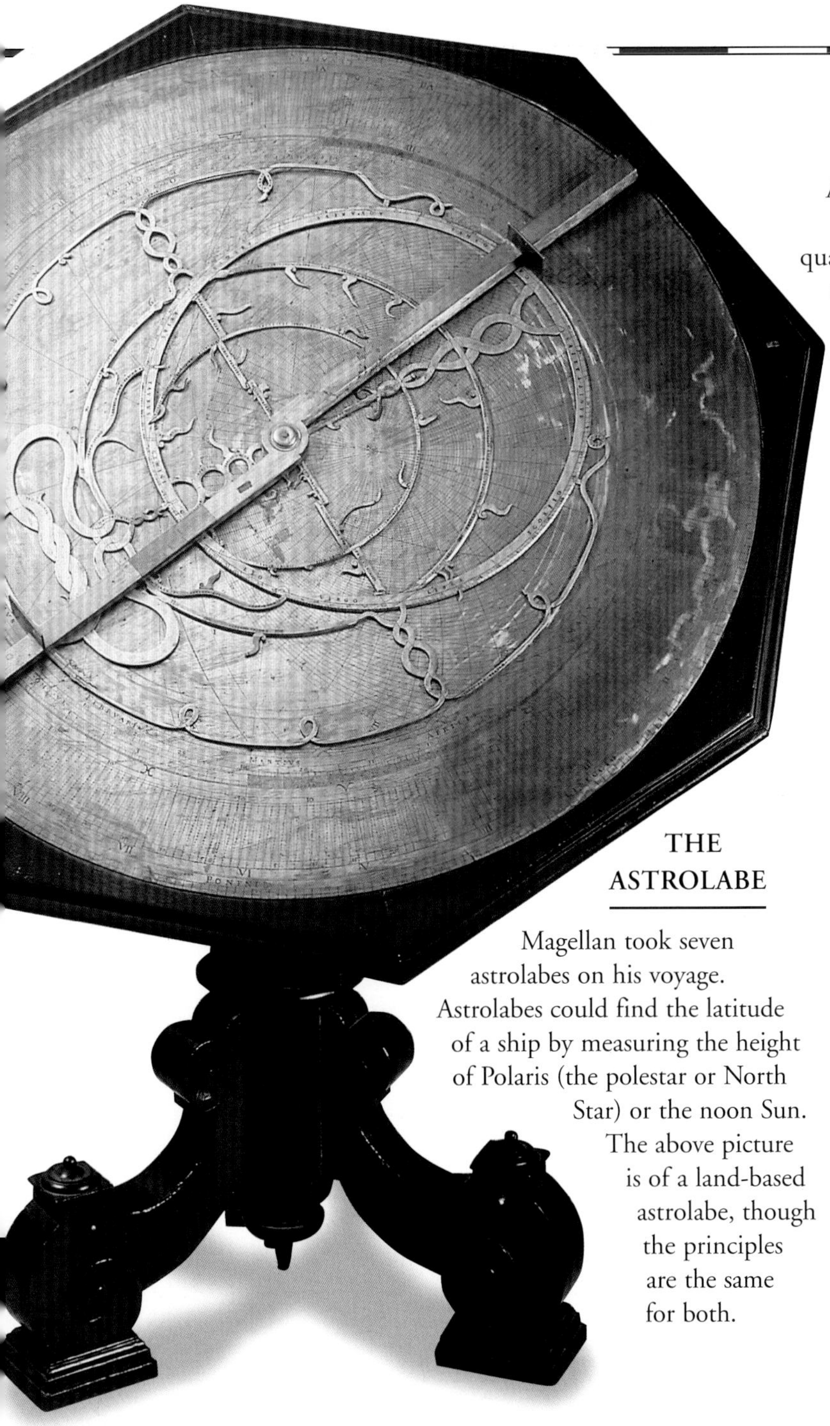

THE QUADRANT

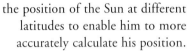

Along with astrolabes, Magellan brought 21 quadrants that measured the angle between the horizon and the Sun or stars, giving the user his latitude position. Magellan also took a set of tables that showed the position of the Sun at different latitudes to enable him to more accurately calculate his position.

THE ASTROLABE

Magellan took seven astrolabes on his voyage. Astrolabes could find the latitude of a ship by measuring the height of Polaris (the polestar or North Star) or the noon Sun. The above picture is of a land-based astrolabe, though the principles are the same for both.

FERDINAND MAGELLAN
-A Timeline-

~1519~

Magellan's ships sail from Spain.

Magellan arrives at the South American coast and then sails on to Rio de Janeiro, Brazil.

~1520~

Magellan reaches San Julián in Argentina and spends the winter there.

Magellan deals with mutiny by his Spanish captains.

WEAPONS ONBOARD

Magellan knew that the voyage he was about to undergo was vulnerable to attack. He prepared for this by taking a large amount of weapons, including 1,000 lances, 60 crossbows, and 120 spears. He also had cannon similar to these (below), although cannon onboard ships did not have wheels at this time.

LANDING IN RIO DE JANEIRO

Three months after setting sail from Spain, Magellan reached the Brazilian coast on December 6, 1519. Magellan was nervous because the entire area was controlled by Portugal. He sailed south until he landed in present-day Rio de Janeiro. After stocking up on fresh supplies, the ships continued south and spent the winter in San Julián, Argentina.

THE SPANISH CAPTAINS MUTINY

After spending the winter in San Julián, Magellan invited all the captains to eat with him. None of them came, and instead they sent a demand that the fleet return to Spain. Magellan acted ruthlessly. The captain of the *Victoria* was killed and others were either imprisoned or abandoned on the shore. In October 1520, as they neared the South Pole, the captain and crew of the *San Antonio* mutinied again and sailed back toward Spain.

AROUND THE TIP OF SOUTH AMERICA

On October 21, 1520, the ships entered what is today known as the Strait of Magellan, although Magellan himself called it *Estrecho de Todos los Santos* (Strait of All Saints'). The strait was a narrow and dangerous channel, and they were sailing straight into the wind. Sometimes the wind was so strong that the ships had to be towed by rowboats. It took 38 days to sail through it. With only three ships left, Magellan eventually reached the Pacific Ocean on November 28, 1520.

SIGHTING STRANGE ANIMALS

Magellan and his men had sailed farther south than any other Europeans, and they saw many different creatures. They caught animals such as seals and penguins for food. Crew member Antonio Pigafetta called the seals "sea wolves," and he thought the penguins were geese. In his diary, he wrote, "These geese are black . . . and they do not fly, and live upon fish. They have beaks like that of a crow."

Setting Off

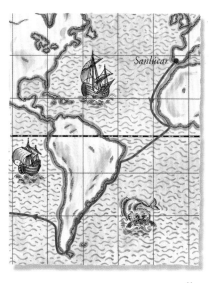

The five ships sailed from Sanlúcar on September 20, 1519, with the *Trinidad* leading the way. An Italian nobleman, Antonio Pigafetta, kept diaries for the whole trip. From these diaries it is clear that Magellan faced many difficulties onboard the ship. The other officers on the voyage disliked Magellan because he was Portuguese and plotted against him. He had to deal with several mutinies. At first he had to treat the crew with care. Pigafetta says that he did not tell them where they were going "so that his men should not from amazement and fear be unwilling to accompany him on so long a voyage." After stopping for supplies at the Canary Islands, Magellan sailed along the West African coast in order to avoid Portuguese patrol ships before setting off across the Atlantic.

SAINT ELMO'S FIRE

The ships hit a huge Atlantic storm. The electrical charge created huge sparks that made the ships' masts appear to be on fire. The crew thought the lights were saints protecting them and called them Saint Elmo's fire.

SEARCHING FOR THE STRAIT

While sailing along the South American coast, Magellan sent ships ahead to search for the route around South America. He explored the entrance to the River Plate, thinking it might be the entrance to the Pacific. The *Santiago* was sunk while searching for the strait, causing even more resentment among his crew.

The Voyage Completed

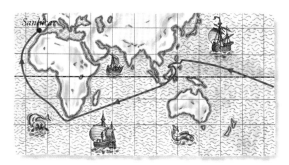

Magellan reached the Pacific Ocean more than one year after leaving Spain. He had put down two mutinies and lost one ship to a rebellious crew, with another wrecked. When the three remaining ships left the strait, they became the first Europeans to sail into the Pacific Ocean. But they were not the first Europeans to see the Pacific Ocean. Vasco de Balboa had this honor—he crossed Central America to the west coast by foot in 1513. Balboa had simply named the ocean the "Great South Sea." Magellan named it the Pacific Ocean because of the gentle winds he found there. Many of his crew wanted to return home, but Magellan believed that it was now only a short trip to Asia. They sailed for three more months, seeing only two uninhabited islands (which they named the Unfortunate Islands) before finally landing in Guam.

THE VAST OCEAN

The three-month trip across the ocean took its toll on the crew. The biscuits had either been eaten by rats or were rotten. The water was too foul for many to drink. The crew was so desperate that they ate sawdust, rats, and strips of leather. Many became very sick with scurvy, and 29 died.

THE DEATH OF MAGELLAN

Cilapulapu, one of the islands of the Philippines, refused to accept Spanish rule. On April 27, 1521, Magellan and 60 armed men tried to subdue Cilapulapu. In the battle that followed, Magellan was hit by a spear and was then hacked to death.

ARRIVAL IN THE PHILIPPINES

It took another week for the fleet to sail from Guam and arrive in the Philippines. There, sick sailors were put ashore to recover, and Magellan began trading with the local inhabitants. In exchange for some of the hawk bells and mirrors that Magellan had brought with him, he was given a basket of ginger and a bar of gold.

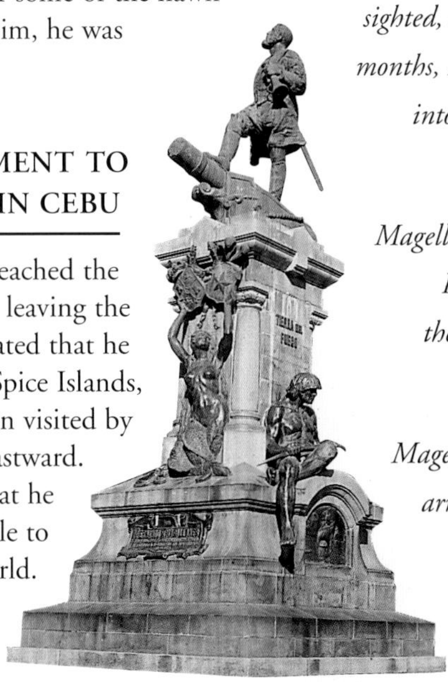

MONUMENT TO MAGELLAN IN CEBU

When Magellan reached the island of Cebu after leaving the Philippines, he calculated that he was now west of the Spice Islands, which had already been visited by Europeans by traveling eastward. It was at this point that he knew it was possible to sail around the world.

LANDING IN GUAM

On March 6, 1521, Magellan reached the island of Guam, part of the modern Mariana Islands. There was obvious relief at reaching land and the opportunity to stock up on fresh supplies. The local people pictured here (left) tried to steal one of their landing boats. Magellan reacted by calling the islands the Ladrones, or Thieves, Islands. He also burned down a village to set an example.

TIERRA DEL FUEGO

Sailing through the Strait of Magellan at night, they saw many fires from distant native camps. They then called the land Tierra del Fuego, the Land of Fire. Once through, the ships remained close together while sailing up the west coast of South America.

THE TRIP HOME

When Magellan was killed, the *Trinidad* and *Victoria* headed back to Spain. Only the *Victoria* completed the voyage home. The trip had brought no profit to the Spanish king, but Magellan had proved that a westward route to Asia did exist.

FERDINAND MAGELLAN
-A Timeline-

~1520~

The strait between the Atlantic and Pacific oceans is sighted, and after several months, Magellan emerges into the Pacific.

~1521~

Magellan lands in Guam. He is killed in the Philippines.

~1522~

Magellan's ship Victoria arrives back in Spain.

Greenland

North
America

Atlantic
Ocean

N

South
America

KEY

—— Drake

DRAKE

Europe

Russia

China

India

Africa

Indian
Ocean

Australia

Antarctica

This map shows the voyage
of Francis Drake.

Francis Drake—the Early Years

*T*he name *Sir Francis Drake* is best identified with England's defeat of the Spanish Armada, his circumnavigation of the world, and stories of heroic raids upon the Spaniards in the Caribbean. As with so many heroes, however, the story is more complex. Francis Drake was born to a humble farming family in Devon, England, and might have become a farmer himself had his father not been an outspoken Protestant lay preacher who was forced to leave his home with his family and seek safe refuge in Kent. They lived for some years onboard a hulk moored on the Medway River, which no doubt fired the imagination of the young Francis. He was apprenticed to the owner and captain of a small coaster that traded between England and Holland. His distant cousin John Hawkins secured him a position as a purser on a slave-trading voyage, and Drake soon rose to the rank of captain.

DEFENDING THE FLEET

When Drake's father arrived in Kent, he became a lay preacher to the seamen in Chatham Dockyard, living with his family on a hulk moored on the Medway River. In 1560, he became the vicar of Upchurch, a nearby small riverside village. The young Francis first learned his seafaring skills on the Medway. The picture above shows Upnor Castle, built by Elizabeth I in 1559–1567 to defend the new dockyard in Chatham.

CHILDHOOD HOME

Francis Drake was born in a small farm cottage in Crowndale, near Tavistock in Devon, some time between 1539 and 1545, the eldest of 12 children. His father, Edmund, had been a sailor but had settled on his brother John's farm in 1544. This statue was later erected in Tavistock in honor of Drake's achievements.

DRAKE'S ISLAND

Following riots by Catholics in the West Country in 1549, Edmund Drake was forced to leave his home with his family and seek refuge on St. Nicholas's Island in Plymouth harbor. From there, his relative William Hawkins arranged for his safe removal to Kent. The island was afterward known as "Drake's Island" to commemorate the event.

LANDED GENTRY

Following his knighthood in 1581, Drake boosted his status by claiming to be descended from a Devonshire landed family of that name. He had their coat of arms displayed aboard his ship the *Golden Hind*.

SIR FRANCIS DRAKE
-A Timeline-

~1541~

The probable year of Francis Drake's birth in Devon, England.

~1547~

King Henry VIII dies and is succeeded by Edward VI.

~1549~

Thomas Cranmer's Book of Common Prayer *is published; leads to Catholic riots.*

Drake family (Protestants) is forced to leave Devon for Kent.

A TRADE OF MISERY

John Hawkins, a prominent figure in Queen Elizabeth's navy, began his illustrious career in 1562 engaged in the slave trade (like Drake himself and many others). Drake's first such voyage was as a purser aboard one of Hawkins's ships in 1566. The voyage itself ended in disaster, but Drake went on to become an officer, serving with Hawkins on a later slave-trading trip, and in 1568, he took command of his first ship.

IRISH REVOLTS

In 1573, on his return from an especially successful raid on Spanish ships in the Caribbean, Drake was obliged to go to Ireland rather than return home. Elizabeth had struck a temporary peace with Spain, and his presence in England would have been an embarrassment. He stayed there for three years, helping Walter Devereux, 1st Earl of Essex, put down Irish opposition to English colonization. The mission failed, eventually leading to open revolt, when many English settlers were killed.

JACQUES CARTIER (1491–1557)

Jacques Cartier was a French explorer, commissioned by the king of France to search for possible sites for new settlements in North America and for a northwest passage. He made several memorable excursions into the waterways around northeast North America and in 1534 circumnavigated the Gulf of Saint Lawrence. This was then thought to be a gateway to the Pacific Ocean but turned out to be a huge bay off eastern Canada. He is seen here (above) on a later expedition in 1542, landing on the banks of the mighty Saint Lawrence River. Cartier's explorations led to later French claims on Canada.

SIR FRANCIS DRAKE
-A Timeline-

~1560~

Edmund Drake (Francis's father) takes up the vicarage of Upchurch, Kent.

~1566~

Drake makes his first voyage to the Caribbean as a junior officer on Hawkins's third slave-trading mission to the Spanish Main.

~1568~

Mary Queen of Scots flees to England in exile.

The Hawkins/Drake slave voyage ends in disaster in San Juan de Ulúa, Mexico.

INHOSPITABLE SEAS

The seas of the North Atlantic and Arctic oceans are very inhospitable. Icebergs are a particular problem, and vast areas ice over completely during the winter. This made it difficult for early explorers to chart the northern coasts of North America and Russia. Ironically, what none of them knew was that the search for both the Northeast and Northwest passages led ultimately to the same place (later named the Bering Strait), which is the only passage into the northern Pacific, between Alaska and Siberia.

The Search for the NE & NW Passages

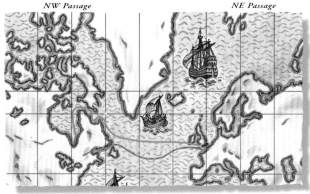
NW Passage   *NE Passage*

■ *Cartier (1534–6)*   ■ *Frobisher (1576)*   ■ *Hudson (1610–11)*

*T*ogether, Spain and Portugal controlled the southern seaways, forcing other nations to search for an alternate route to reach the Pacific Ocean and the fabled riches of China and Southeast Asia. Two possibilities emerged: the Northeast Passage, traversing the northern coasts of Russia, and the Northwest Passage, passing around the northern coasts of North America. Drake himself tried unsuccessfully to locate the Northwest Passage, from the Pacific side, in 1578. Having completed his mission to attack Spanish ports on the west coast of South America, he struck north to find a way home but was forced back across the Pacific and sailed home around the world, though that was never his original intention. Several navigators in succeeding centuries managed to locate the strait between Alaska and Russia, but none was able to pass through it from the northwest. Norwegian explorer Roald Amundsen is generally accepted to be the first person to sail around northern Canada and through the Bering Strait, in 1906, after a three-year expedition.

THE FUR TRADE

Denied the lucrative markets of China and the Far East, merchants soon realized the potential of the fur (and later gold) to be found in North America. Large companies were established, such as the Hudson Bay Company, which made huge profits by buying animal pelts from the Native Americans at very low prices and then exporting them to Europe.

HENRY HUDSON

Henry Hudson was an English navigator and explorer who was employed by the Dutch East India Company to search for the Northwest Passage. After several attempts, he reached the North American coast and discovered what are now known as the Hudson River, Strait, and Bay. In 1611, after a winter spent ice bound, his crew mutinied and cast him adrift in a small boat, along with eight others, and he was never seen again.

NEAR MISS

One of the problems facing 16th-century explorers was that the lands for which they were searching were complete unknown quantities, both in terms of location and size. When we trace the routes they followed, we can see just how close they sometimes got to their objectives, without ever realizing it. On his return trip home around the world, for example, Drake sailed a zigzag course through the East Indies in a vain search for the Southern Continent, taking him tantalizingly close to Australia's northern coast.

SIR FRANCIS DRAKE
-A Timeline-

~1569~

Drake marries Mary Newman in St. Budeaux, near Plymouth, England.

~1570~

Drake sails for the coast of Panama and begins his reign of terror among Spanish shipping.

~1576~

Drake returns from Ireland and plans his attack on the west coast of South America (which became his circumnavigation voyage).

~1577~

Drake sets out on his voyage around the world.

~1579~

Drake captures his greatest prize, the Spanish treasure ship Cacafuego.

TRAVELING IN STYLE

Drake's ship on his circumnavigation was originally called the *Pelican*, but he renamed it *Golden Hind* off South America, before attempting his epic voyage across the southern oceans. This was in honor of his patron, Sir Christopher Hatton, whose coat of arms included a hind (a female deer). Drake enjoyed good living and often brought musicians to entertain him on the long months spent aboard his ship.

CENTER OF THE UNIVERSE

In Elizabethan times, the other planets in our solar system were thought to revolve around Earth. Armillary spheres were used to demonstrate the movements of the heavenly bodies and to show the relative positions of the equator, the Tropics, and the Arctic and Antarctic circles. After Magellan's expedition successfully circumnavigated the world, it became possible to more accurately calculate Earth's size and to draw more precise navigational charts.

THE FIRST ENGLISHMAN IN JAPAN

Elizabethan pilot and adventurer Will Adams set sail in 1598 with a Dutch expedition to Southeast Asia. Only one of the five ships that set out survived, blowing off course and eventually landing in Japan in 1600. Adams was taken prisoner but was later released on the condition that he taught the Japanese his seafaring skills. James Clavell's novel *Shogun* is based on Adams's exploits.

Quest for the Southern Continent

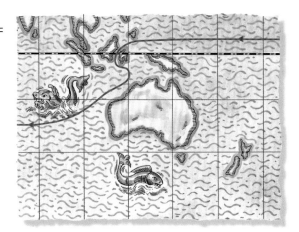

While few Europeans suspected the existence of North and South America in the 1500s (China was believed to lie due west across the Atlantic Ocean), legends abounded of a vast "Southern Continent" somewhere in the South Atlantic, which many presumed to be the fabled lost island of Atlantis. Several attempts at discovery were made, including by Drake on the return voyage of his circumnavigation. Explorers hoped to discover an inhabited and highly civilized land where they could trade, but it remained elusive. At the same time, merchant adventurers were also looking to forge trading links with Southeast Asia, in particular the Spice Islands (now the Moluccas in Indonesia), China, and Japan. The first Englishman to set foot in Japan was Will Adams. Born in Gillingham, Kent, he learned his seafaring skills on the Medway River, like Drake before him.

By the end of the 1500s, Spain's golden age was coming to a close. Most of the discoveries made after then were by English, Dutch, and French expeditions.

ELUSIVE CONTINENT

Although a few explorers had made brief contact with the islands to the north of Australia, the existence of an inhabited Southern Continent eluded the Elizabethans. Abel Tasman landed in Australia in 1642 (right), but it was not until the voyages of Captain James Cook, in 1768–1780, that the existence of a vast habitable continent (where we now know Antarctica to be) was finally disproved and the full outline of Australia confirmed.

Drake's Circumnavigation of the World

rancis Drake was only the second commander (and the first Englishman) to successfully circumnavigate the world. The main reason for Drake's epic journey, however, was not in the interests of scientific discovery but of trade and plunder, motivated by greed. At the time, Spain was the most powerful nation in Europe, and jealously guarded the seaways to her lucrative new colonies. Queen Elizabeth I commissioned Drake to sail across the southern Atlantic, through the Strait of Magellan, and attack Spanish treasure ships and settlements on South America's unprotected west coast. Drake then went on to cross the Pacific Ocean and reach the Spice Islands of the East Indies. Drake returned home a rich man, his successful circumnavigation being little more than a boost to his reputation.

"THE DRAGON"

Drake was a powerful personality and commanded respect wherever he went. Native peoples often paid homage to him, and even the Spanish grudgingly referred to him as *El Draque*, the Dragon, supposedly blessed with magical powers.

LOST CIVILIZATION

The Maya civilization of Central America flourished many centuries before Drake's circumnavigation. They evolved a sophisticated knowledge of astronomy and mathematics, but there is no evidence that Drake brought back any scientific discoveries from the cities he visited; like the Spanish, he merely plundered their riches. The round tower shown here is an observatory in the Mexican city of Chichén Itzá.

SPANISH GOLD

The Spaniards ruthlessly exploited the nations of Central and South America, plundering their riches. They melted down gold ornaments and put the natives to work in gold and silver mines. The wealth they shipped back to Spain aroused the interest of Drake and other Elizabethan privateers. The coins shown here are doubloons (meaning a double, or two-escudo, piece), the highest-value Spanish coins at that time.

NEW ALBION

Drake stopped in what is now San Francisco, California, to resupply his ships before commencing the return trip home. He had an audience with the local Native Americans, who invited him to become their king. He refused but did claim the area for England (calling it New Albion), though no English settlement was ever established there. The Spanish, who made several explorations up the Californian coast, established a small missionary settlement by the bay, which they called San Francisco.

REPRISALS

The dangers of native reprisals facing Drake and other explorers (and the Spanish settlers) were always present. Here, Brazilian cannibals allow missionaries to baptize their prisoners, but only with a damp cloth so as not to spoil the flavor.

AZTEC SPLENDOR

This picture of Tenochtitlán, Mexico, shows a preconquest view of the magnificent Aztec capital city. Although Drake never reached this far inland (concentrating his efforts on coastal ports), he was just as guilty as the Spaniards in plundering the riches of such ancient sites, especially gold.

SIR FRANCIS DRAKE
-A TIMELINE-

~1580~

Drake returns from his circumnavigation of the world.

Queen Elizabeth I is excommunicated by the pope.

~1581~

Drake is knighted aboard his ship the Golden Hind.

Drake buys Buckland Abbey.

Drake is appointed mayor of Plymouth.

~1585~

Drake sacks Santiago, Cape Verde.

Drake sets sail for the West Indies, his first command as admiral.

~1587~

Mary Queen of Scots is executed.

The Spanish decide to launch an offensive against England.

Drake sacks the port of Cádiz, Spain—"singeing the king of Spain's beard."

SIR FRANCIS DRAKE
-A Timeline-

~1588~

The Spanish Armada is sent against England and is defeated in the English Channel after a weeklong running battle.

~1595~

Drake sets off to attack Puerto Rico (his last voyage) with Sir John Hawkins.

Sir John Hawkins dies.

~1596~

Drake dies of dysentery in Puerto Bello, Panama.

SEARCH FOR A WAY HOME

There is some argument surrounding the exact route home taken by Drake. Some claim that he did not touch land again after leaving Java until arriving back in Plymouth. Others believe he may have visited southern India before crossing the Indian Ocean. He is seen here supposedly paying homage to an Indian ruler.

THE *GOLDEN HIND*

Drake set sail from Plymouth on December 13, 1577 with five ships and a combined crew of 164. The flagship was the *Pelican*, a relatively small vessel of 120 tons carrying just 18 cannon. The smallest ship, the *Benedict*, displaced just 15 tons, a tiny vessel to undertake so arduous a journey. Around halfway into the trip, Drake abandoned two of his ships (probably because of high mortality among the crews). Of the other three, the *Marigold* perished and the *Elizabeth*, unbeknown to Drake, returned to England without completing the voyage. Only the flagship, renamed the *Golden Hind*, completed the circumnavigation.

KNIGHTHOOD

On Francis Drake's return from his circumnavigation of the world (1577–1780), he was given a hero's welcome. He was knighted aboard his ship the *Golden Hind* by Elizabeth I the following year.

ILL FEELING

The serpent and beasts shown here are taken from a collection of engravings made to commemorate Drake's epic voyage. The serpent is a universal symbol of evil and bad luck, especially among sailors. Drake's men would have encountered several on the trip, especially when making landfall in South America, which would have made them feel very ill at ease. Drake kept his intended destination a secret from his men, but when they eventually realized the truth, discontent spread throughout the crews. They were incited to mutiny by Drake's one-time friend Thomas Doughty, who was put on trial and executed.

Drake's Circumnavigation of the World

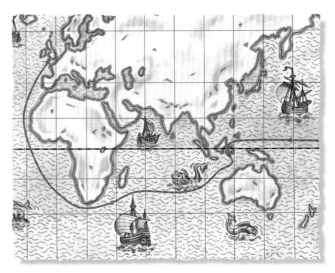

Although usually credited as the second person to sail around the world (after Magellan, 1519–1521), Drake actually deserves more credit for his feat than he is sometimes given. Magellan was the first European to cross the Pacific Ocean, but he never completed the circumnavigation of the world himself, though 18 members of his expedition did return to Spain aboard his ship the *Victoria*. It now seems likely that Magellan's original intention was simply to sail to the East Indies via the Pacific and that it became necessary to return home around the world only to escape attacks from the Portuguese. He was killed in the Philippines after completing around half the journey, which means that Drake was the first commander to successfully complete a circumnavigation himself.

EXOTIC NEW FOODS

It was impossible for Drake to take onboard all the supplies he needed for his voyage, so rations were supplemented en route with exotic foods, such as the pineapple, which is a native fruit of Central and South America. Other foods from the tropics included coconuts, bananas, and tomatoes. Drake brought these foods, among many others, back to England, where they quickly became sought as delicacies at the table. Some foods could be grown in England, but pineapples could survive only in conservatories. Pineapples also became a favorite model for architectural features.

SECRET VOYAGE

Shortly before embarking on his epic voyage, Drake was summoned to a secret meeting with Queen Elizabeth. She apparently instructed him to raid the unprotected Spanish ports on the west coast of South America. To that end, Drake was extremely successful and brought his investors an incredible 4,700 percent profit. Elizabeth herself profited by $440,000. Drake's first words when he returned to Plymouth on September 26, 1580 were, reputedly, "Does the queen still live?"

PITCHED BATTLE

The commander of the English fleet sent to stop the Armada was Lord Howard of Effingham. A weeklong pitched battle took place in the English Channel, but the English could not halt the progress of the Spanish. The battle turned in favor of the English, however, when Drake launched eight fire ships into the Armada off Gravelines (north of Calais, Fance), which threw the Spanish into disarray. The following day, the Armada was routed and fled into the North Sea.

The Spanish Armada

Following Henry VIII's break with the Church of Rome in 1533, England was under constant threat from the Catholic countries of Europe to reestablish papal authority. Spain was especially enraged at the acts of open piracy on her ships by English adventurers, particularly during Elizabeth I's reign, and needed little persuading to launch an offensive against England. In July 1588, a massive armada of 138 ships and 24,000 men was sent to invade England.

ARMADA MEDAL

This gold medal, commemorating England's victory over the Armada, was awarded to each of the commanders of the English fleet.

THE ARMADA APPROACHES

According to an unsubstantiated legend, Drake is supposed to have insisted on finishing his game of lawn bowling before setting out to sea. The Spanish Armada created a formidable spectacle as it advanced slowly up the English Channel. The English fleet was hampered by the tide in rapidly getting its ships into open waters, but the daring seamanship of Drake, Vice Admiral John Hawkins, Martin Frobisher, and many others eventually saved the day.

Drake's Later Life

DRAKE'S LAST VOYAGE

Drake's last ill-fated voyage took place in 1595–1596. He and John Hawkins were commanded to attack Puerto Rico in order to cut off Spain's supply of treasure ships. There was friction between the two admirals from the start, which came to a head when Drake decided to make an excursion to the Canary Islands (above) for supplies. The attack failed, but worse was to come.

A messenger ship was sent from the Canaries to warn the governor of Puerto Rico of the intended attack. The island's defenses had been sadly lacking and would probably have succumbed to Drake and Hawkins. But with two weeks' warning, the Spaniards were able to make the necessary preparations, and the English attack failed dismally.

Hawkins died before the attack was launched and Drake around one month later, of dysentery, on January 25, 1596, off Puerto Bello, Panama.

Although Drake has often been accused of being a ne'er-do-well who was little better that a legalized pirate, acting as Elizabeth's agent in her war with Spain, such criticism is perhaps a little harsh. He was, by all accounts, an honorable man who took good care of his crews, even if he sometimes used rough methods. He certainly hankered after the finer things in life and, following his knighthood in 1581, regarded himself as a member of the new aristocracy. This earned him many enemies among those with inherited titles. After his circumnavigation, he became the mayor of Plymouth and campaigned for many improvements to the town, including a better water supply. A short man of stocky build, he is said to have become quite plump in later life and settled into semiretirement at Buckland Abbey, near his birthplace. This had been seized by the crown at the dissolution and converted into a fine house by Sir Richard Grenville.

"DRAKE'S DRUM"

"Take my drum to England, hang et by the shore,
Strike et when your powder's runnin' low;
If the Dons sight Devon, I'll quit the port o' Heaven,
An' drum them up the Channel as we drummed them long ago."

These lines are an extract from a poem by Sir Henry Newbolt. The drum was used aboard the *Golden Hind* to muster the crew for battle. On his deathbed, Drake, according to legend, promised to return and fight for England if ever the drum was beaten at the approach of an enemy.

BRILLIANT STRATEGIST

Throughout his illustrious career, Drake had struck fear into the hearts of the Spaniards. In 1587, he executed a flawless attack on Cádiz harbour, where he was said to have "singed the king of Spain's beard" by destroying 37 (the Spanish claimed it was 24) galleons that were gathering to form an armada to be sent against England. The following year, of course, he was instrumental in defeating the "Great Armada" itself, and in between times he was a constant threat to Spanish shipping in the Caribbean. An expert navigator, he revolutionized naval strategy by taking the fight to the enemy. When Philip II of Spain heard the news of his death, he is said to have openly rejoiced.

FALL FROM FAVOR

In 1583, Drake's first wife died, and soon after he married Elizabeth Sydenham, who outlived him, but he had no children by either wife. He engaged in a few expeditions following his circumnavigation, but he slipped gradually into semiretirement following the defeat of the Armada in 1588 and spent more and more time either in London, at court, or in his new official duties in Plymouth. During that time, he fell from favor, and Martin Frobisher superseded him as Queen Elizabeth's shining star.

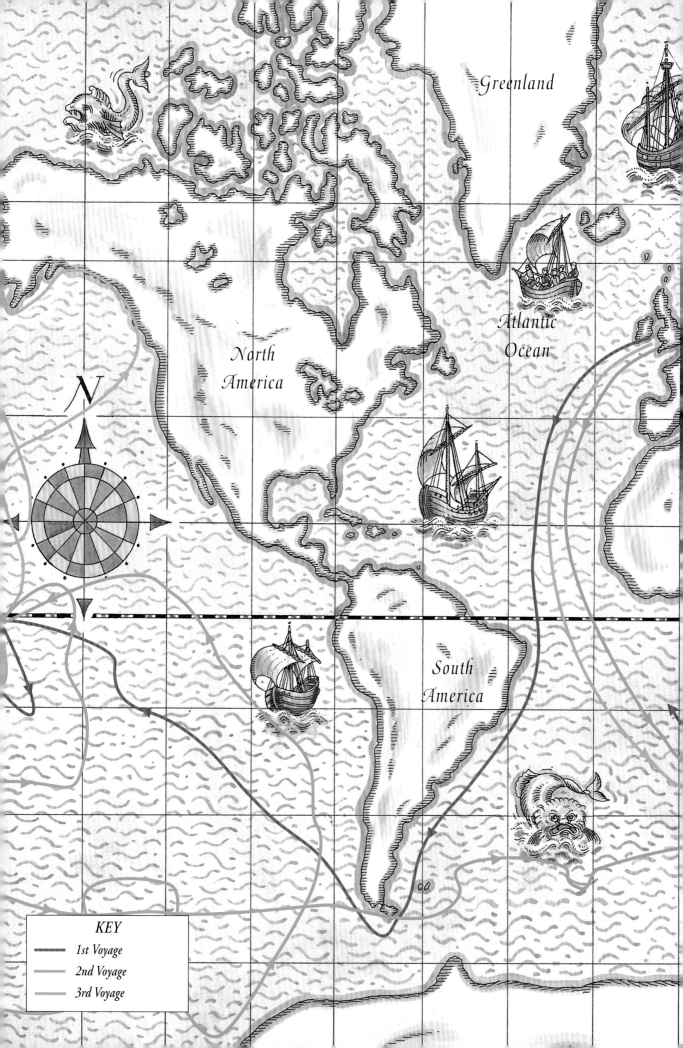

Greenland

Atlantic
Ocean

North
America

N

South
America

KEY
1st Voyage
2nd Voyage
3rd Voyage

CAPTAIN COOK

Europe

Russia

Africa

China

India

Indian
Ocean

Australia

This map shows the voyages
of James Cook.

Antarctica

Cook's Origins & Early Life

James Cook was born in a two-room cottage in Marton-in-Cleveland, north Yorkshire, England, on October 7, 1728. His father was a Scottish-born laborer, his mother a Yorkshire woman, and they had seven children, of whom four died before they reached the age of five. James helped his father on a farm in Great Ayton before being apprenticed to a grocer and haberdasher in Staithes. Not liking retail work, in 1746 he was apprenticed to John Walker, a Whitby ship owner and captain in the coal trade, and spent the next nine years sailing from the Tyne River to London and the Baltic. Walker wanted to make him master of a ship, but instead, in

1755, Cook volunteered for the Royal Navy.

UNLOADING A COLLIER

Shipping coal was a difficult physical trade. Ships were loaded and unloaded by manpower. Coal had to be handled in baskets and is shown here being "whipped," or tipped down a chute. Cook managed these men and such work on the Tyne and Thames rivers.

JAMES COOK, AGED 48

Cook became a naval captain and explorer of world fame. But his navigational ability was based on seafaring skills learned as a youth in the coal trade in the North Sea.

THE CUSTOMS HOUSE, LONDON

The London Customs House would have been well known to Cook. Although only cargo shipped from overseas was subject to an import duty, coal from northeast England, carried down the east coast, still had to be declared.

THE PORT OF WHITBY

Whitby, where Cook went to sea, is on the northeast coast of England, where coal mining close to the coast and the Tyne River made its shipments to London an important trade. Colliers were beached for loading and repairs.

A NORTH SEA COLLIER

This model of a "cat-built bark" shows the type of ship used in the coal trade. A strong, roomy hull permitted it to rest on a beach or riverbed and carry a lot of cargo.

CAPTAIN JAMES COOK
-A Timeline-

~1728~

Cook is born in Marton-in-Cleveland, north Yorkshire, England.

~1745~

Cook works for a grocer and haberdasher in Staithes.

Master's Mate

Great Britain was on the verge of war with France in June 1755 when Cook joined the 60-gun ship *Eagle* in Spithead, off Portsmouth. One month later, he was rated a "master's mate." Two years later, he become a ship's master himself, sailing in the 64-gun *Pembroke* to assist the British in driving the French out of Canada. During the winter of 1758–1759, Cook helped perfect a chart of the Saint Lawrence River, which permitted an expedition under General James Wolfe to seize Quebec. At the mouth of the river, the waters around the island of Newfoundland were valuable for their cod, and after the war, each summer until 1767, Cook was employed to make charts of the island.

A SEAMAN HEAVING THE LEAD

As the master of a warship, Cook would have often relied on seamen sounding the depth of water beneath the ship's keel by casting a lead weight on a line over the side.

CHART OF NEWFOUNDLAND

This was one of the highly accurate charts made by James Cook and Michael Lane between 1763 and 1767. Cook did the surveying for these charts each summer, returning to London every winter to prepare the finished products for publication. Cook had married Elizabeth Betts in 1762 and lived in East London.

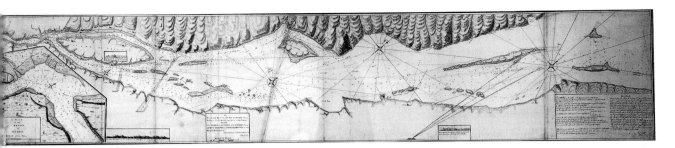

COOK'S CHART OF THE SAINT LAWRENCE RIVER

The chart Cook prepared in 1758–1759 shows the numerous islands and shoals around which the army transports and naval escorts had to navigate in order to reach Quebec. Cook's chart opened the way for the defeat of the French on the Heights of Abraham, which led to British possession of Canada.

CAPTAIN JAMES COOK
-A TIMELINE-

~1746~

Cook is apprenticed to a Whitby ship owner and coal trader.

~1755~

Cook volunteers for the Royal Navy.

~1756~

The Seven Years' War starts between Great Britain and France.

~1757~

Cook becomes a master in the Royal Navy.

~1759~

Cook perfects a chart of the Saint Lawrence River.

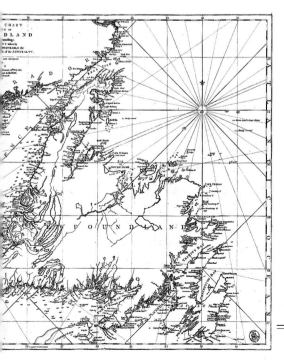

THE DEATH OF WOLFE IN QUEBEC

General Wolfe was shot in the battle for Quebec on September 13, 1759 and died after hearing of his victory. He was only 32 years old. His body is buried in Greenwich, England, where he lived and where his statue now stands in Greenwich park.

THEODOLITE, 1737

When Cook charted Newfoundland, he worked in conjunction with surveyors led by Joseph Des Barres making maps onshore. Surveying instruments were already sophisticated. Theodolites, used for measuring angles, had telescopic sights and rack-work circles for both the vertical and horizontal movements.

~1759~
*General Wolfe takes
Quebec, Canada.*

~1762~
*Cook marries Elizabeth Betts
and lives in East London.*

~1763~
*Cook begins charting the
coastline of Newfoundland.*

~1768~
*Cook is chosen to command
the ship to carry observers
of the transit of Venus.*

A Pacific Voyage

Cook was fortunate that his skills at navigation, surveying, and chart making were noticed by Sir Hugh Palliser, another Yorkshireman, who was twice Cook's captain and subsequently governor of Newfoundland, comptroller of the navy, and a member of the Board of Admiralty directed by Lord Sandwich. The latter presented Cook to King George III, who was very interested in scientific discoveries. In fact, in 1768, when the Royal Society wanted to measure the distance of Earth from the Sun by observing the "transit of Venus" from somewhere in the southern Pacific, he helped finance the voyage. Cook was chosen to captain the ship sent to carry the scientists, led by Joseph Banks, who later held the role of president of the Royal Society for 40 years.

BANKS'S COLLECTIONS

As well as sailing with Cook to New Zealand and Australia, Banks traveled to Newfoundland and Iceland to develop his collection of natural history specimens. The collection became a foundation of the one in the Natural History Museum in London.

JOSEPH BANKS

A wealthy young gentleman, Banks joined Cook's first voyage of exploration in the Pacific to pursue his natural history interests. He was president of the Royal Society from 1778 until 1820 and helped publish the journals of Cook's last voyage.

LORD SANDWICH

Although better known for his indulgence in London life—his name was given to the food he reputedly ordered to avoid leaving the gambling table—Sandwich was an accomplished administrator and First Lord of the Admiralty from 1770 until 1782. In this role, he promoted Cook after his second voyage and encouraged him to volunteer for a third. As Cook's letter to him in 1776 suggests, they became good friends, and after Cook's death, Sandwich presided over the publication of his journals.

ASTRONOMER AT HIS TRANSIT INSTRUMENT

The Astronomer Royal predicted the Transit of Venus across the face of the Sun in 1769 from repeated observations at the Royal Observatory, founded in 1675 in Greenwich, England. From there, nightly observations mapped the visible universe.

GEORGE III

George III became king in 1760 at the height of the Seven Years' War with France. He had a political, as well as scientific, interest in encouraging exploration, as France was intent on enlarging her empire. Significantly, though Cook's last voyage was overshadowed by the rebellion of George III's American colonies, his journals for the voyage were published on the king's 48th birthday.

LUNAR DISTANCE TABLE FROM THE FIRST *NAUTICAL ALMANAC*

This *Almanac*, "just published," contained the angular distances between the Moon and seven selected stars for 1767 and permitted Cook to calculate his longitude and make charts with unprecedented accuracy.

[48]   APRIL 1767.

Distances of ☽'s Center from ☉, and from Stars west of her.

Days	Stars Names	12 Hours	15 Hours	18 Hours	21 Hours
		° ' ''	° ' ''	° ' ''	° ' ''
1	The Sun.	40. 59. 11	42. 34. 44	44. 9. 51	45. 44. 4
2		53. 32. 7	55. 4. 24	56. 36. 16	58. 7. 4
3		65. 39. 18	67. 8. 27	68. 37. 14	70. 5. 30
4		77. 22. 36	78. 48. 58	80. 15. 1	81. 40. 40
5		88. 45. 20	90. 9. 27	91. 33. 21	92. 57.
6		99. 52. 6	101. 14. 34	102. 36. 52	103. 59.
7		110. 47. 42	112. 9. 6	113. 30. 25	114. 51. 4
6	Aldebaran	50. 36. 10	52. 4. 5	53. 31. 57	54. 59. 4
7		62. 17. 43	63. 45. 10	65. 12. 34	66. 39. 5
8	Pollux.	31. 25. 48	32. 53. 11	34. 20. 40	35. 48. 1
9		43. 7. 5	44. 35. 4	46. 3. 8	47. 31. 1
10	Regulus.	17. 51. 57	19. 20. 36	20. 49. 26	22. 18. 2
11		29. 45. 36	31. 15. 26	32. 45. 26	34. 15. 3
12		41. 48. 49	43. 19. 55	44. 54. 10	46. 22. 3
13		54. 2. 11	55. 34. 36	57. 7. 12	58. 39. 5
14		66. 26. 28	68. 0. 18	69. 34. 20	71. 8. 3
15	Spica ♍	25. 4. 34	26. 39. 23	28. 14. 26	29. 49. 4
16		37. 49. 37	39. 26. 14	41. 3. 5	42. 40.
17		50. 48. 40	52. 26. 59	54. 5. 31	55. 44.
18		64. 1. 2	65. 41. 3	67. 21. 18	69. 1. 4
20	Antares.	31. 37. 14	33. 19. 7	35. 1. 13	36. 43. 3
21		45. 18. 29	47. 2. 10	48. 46. 5	50. 30.
22		59. 14. 6	60. 59. 31	62. 45. 11	64. 31.
23		73. 23. 37	75. 10. 43	76. 58. 2	78. 45. 3
23	♑ Capricorni.	33. 17. 26	35. 4. 38	36. 52. 4	38. 39. 4
24		47. 41. 9	49. 29. 53	51. 18. 44	53. 7. 4
25	α Aquilæ.	65. 57. 35	67. 29. 54	69. 2. 36	70. 35. 3
26		78. 24. 51	79. 55. 9	81. 33. 29	83. 7. 4

A MODEL OF THE *ENDEAVOUR*

This model demonstrates what the *Endeavour* looked like when she was purchased in 1768. Previously named the *Earl of Pembroke*, she weighed 369 tons and cost $4,200. She was armed with six carriage guns and eight swivel guns. With her large storage capacity, she carried 12 months' supply of all provisions except beer, of which there was enough for one month. Most supplies were stored in the hold, and when fully laden, her draft was 14 ft. (4.3m).

DOLLOND TELESCOPE

Cook applied to the Admiralty for a supply of navigational, chart-making, and astronomical instruments. Advances in the design of these instruments gave him the ability to navigate accurately and record his discoveries for posterity. His navigational instruments included a telescope like this one made by Peter Dollond of London, who made the best available at the time. Since the 1750s, telescopes had been made with an achromatic object glass that reduced their size and rendered objects almost free of color distortion.

Preparations

In April 1768, the Admiralty purchased the *Endeavour*, a three-year-old Whitby collier like those that Cook had already sailed in the North Sea. She was only 106 ft. (32.3m) long on her upper deck, but her hull was strong enough to rest onshore to receive repairs and capacious enough, with some squeezing, to carry 94 people, provisions, and equipment. While she was repaired in Deptford Dockyard, Cook obtained navigational equipment, including the first *Nautical Almanac*, published by the Astronomer Royal in 1766. Meanwhile, the Royal Society appointed naturalists to collect plants, artists to record what they saw, and an astronomer to observe the transit of Venus.

DECK PLANS OF THE *ENDEAVOUR*

In the navy, the ships' officers and senior civilians generally exercised on the quarterdeck. To accommodate the extra passengers, the decks of the *Endeavour* were subdivided into more cabins. The crew and civilian servants slept in hammocks slung above stores on the lower deck. The hold, containing further provisions, was reached through hatches covered by grates.

CAPTAIN JAMES COOK
-A TIMELINE-

~1766~

The first Nautical Almanac *is published by the Astronomer Royal.*

~1768~

A Whitby collier is purchased by the navy for Cook's voyage and is renamed Endeavour.

The Endeavour *sails for Tahiti.*

COOK'S SEXTANT

Oceanic navigation demanded an instrument that accurately measured the altitude of heavenly bodies. The back staff, invented by John Davis in 1590, was still in use but had been improved upon by John Hadley in 1734 with his quadrant and octant, and by the sextant in 1757. Cook took this sextant, made by Jesse Ramsden of London in around 1770, on his third voyage.

LAUNCHING A SHIP FROM DEPTFORD DOCKYARD

When the *Endeavour* was docked in Deptford, her hull was given an extra skin of wooden sheathing, her masts and yards were replaced, and partitions for extra cabins were inserted. After being refloated, she was rigged and equipped from the great storehouse. Food supplies were obtained from the Deptford provisions yard.

Endeavour

Cook's ship for his first voyage was sold in 1775 and broken up in 1793. For many years there had been attempts to build a replica, which was finally achieved in Fremantle, Australia, between 1988 and 1994. She was built to the official plans in the National Maritime Museum in the U.K., mostly by 18th-century methods but using Australian timber and some modern techniques and artificial materials to enhance the security of the construction and rigging. Here she is shown over the Great Barrier Reef—which her predecessor struck in 1770—and on her voyage to Great Britain in 1997.

SAILING THE *ENDEAVOUR*

Men set the sails as they did more than 200 years ago. The rigging employs more than 700 pulleys called blocks. Here, a seaman frees a snag on the mainsail.

FURNITURE AND EQUIPMENT

The Great Cabin (left) was shared by Cook with the naturalists and was where they did most of their botanical work. The officers' mess (right) has a folding table copied from one owned by Cook. Everything looks as it once did.

CAPTAIN JAMES COOK
-A TIMELINE-

~1769~

The transit of Venus is observed from Tahiti.

Endeavour searches for the Great Southern Continent.

Cook discovers and starts charting New Zealand.

~1770~

Cook sails up the east coast of Australia.

PORTABLE ASTRONOMICAL QUADRANT

To obtain an accurate measurement of the transit of Venus, the observer's latitude and longitude had to be known precisely. Such accuracy could be achieved, with other observations, by using a quadrant to measure the angular distance of the Sun, the Moon, or a star from the zenith, the point immediately overhead. This 12-in. (30.5-cm) portable quadrant, made by John Bird in around 1768, is believed to have been used by Cook on his first voyage.

PORTABLE OBSERVATORY

All the astronomical observations were made from a wood and canvas observatory, designed by John Smeaton (who built the Eddystone Lighthouse in Cornwall, England) and constructed under the eye of Nevil Maskelyne, the astronomer royal.

COOK'S CHART OF NEW ZEALAND

Cook charted the North and South Islands so exactly that their shapes, as he represented them, are almost identical to those derived from modern mapping techniques. Almost all the place names he proposed are still in use today.

QUEEN CHARLOTTE SOUND, NEW ZEALAND

After charting North Island, New Zealand, Cook anchored in this deep coastal inlet, swathed in forest, with abundant supplies of fresh water, fish, wild celery, and scurvy grass. The local Maori, 300–400 in number, were poorer than those in the north. They introduced themselves with a shower of stones, and were obviously cannibals, but soon became friendly.

The Transit of Venus & New Zealand

The First Voyage, 1768–1771

Cook and his companions set sail to observe the transit of Venus in July 1768. They headed for Tahiti, an island in the Pacific discovered by Captain Samuel Wallis, who had just returned from circumnavigating the globe before they set sail. The observations were successfully accomplished in June 1769, when Cook followed secret orders to look for the Great Southern Continent. Exploring south and west, the *Endeavour* discovered New Zealand, which Cook sailed all around. Repairs were made in Queen Charlotte Sound, where the Maori were friendly and helpful. The charts that Cook were to produce would not be improved for another 100 years.

ASTRONOMICAL CLOCK

In 1769, observers of the transit of Venus in different parts of the world had to note the time that the planet appeared to touch the disk of the Sun. Accuracy of timing was essential. Thus, when observations were made, a regulating clock was set up inside the portable observatory onshore. The clock was also used to check the running of marine chronometers. Its own accuracy had been checked by the astronomer royal in Greenwich before the voyage. The clock shown here went on at least one of Cook's voyages and is inscribed "Royal Society No. 35, John Shelton, London."

GREGORIAN REFLECTING TELESCOPE

To ensure accurate and comparable observations of the transit of Venus, the Royal Society issued similar telescopes to all the observers it posted to different parts of the world. This reflecting telescope was made in 1763 in London by James Short. Cook was equipped with two of them.

Australia

The First Voyage, 1768–1771

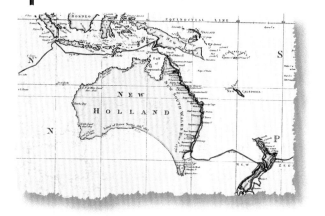

Cook sailed west from New Zealand to explore Australia. Dutchmen had discovered the west coast, which they named New Holland, and the island of Tasmania more than 150 years before. But the east coast was still unknown. Sighting its southern end, Cook sailed north, stopping in a bay so full of specimens for the naturalists that they called it Botany Bay. Farther north, the *Endeavour* suddenly struck part of the Great Barrier Reef. Getting off with difficulty, the ship had to be beached for six weeks for repairs. Before sailing home, Cook claimed the whole coast of New South Wales for King George III.

AUSTRALIAN FISH

Fish caught by the seamen and naturalists were both eaten and studied. The former enthusiastically helped the latter. The *Arripis Trutta*, shown here, grows to 3 ft. (1m) long and is found in the waters of Australia and New Zealand.

A KANGAROO

While resting in the Endeavour River, they saw animals "about the size of a greyhound, slender, mouse colored, swift, with a long tail, jumping like a hare." They outpaced Banks's greyhound, but several were shot and eaten. This one was painted by Sydney Parkinson.

THE *ENDEAVOUR* UNDER REPAIR

After the *Endeavour* got off the Great Barrier Reef, Cook found the Endeavour River, where the ship could be unloaded and beached for the repair of her hull.

AUSTRALIAN FLOWER

While the *Endeavour* was
being repaired, Joseph Banks
gathered more specimens of
plants and flowers, which
were later presented to the
British Museum. This one
is called *Solanum viride*.

BOTANY BAY

Cook's first landing on Australian soil was in Botany
Bay, where most of the vegetation and bird and
animal life were quite new. They met Aborigines and
caught large stingrays. Cook named the bay after the
large quantity of botanical specimens collected by
Joseph Banks and botanist Daniel Solander.

QUARTERDECK OF A NAVAL
VESSEL IN THE TROPICS

To shelter a ship's officers from the
sun, canvas awnings were rigged over
the quarterdeck. Common seamen
were excluded from this deck unless
performing some duty. Animals,
taken to supply food, often became
pets. This picture was painted in
around 1775 on a voyage from the West Indies to England,
but the quarterdeck of the *Endeavour* probably looked
similar as she made her way up the east coast of Australia.
Note the goat (for milk). Cook also took one—which had
already sailed once around the world with Wallis!

The Great Southern Continent
The Second Voyage, 1772–1775

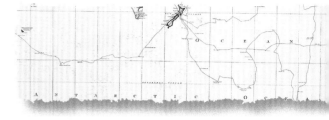

Cook's first voyage had not disproved the existence of a Great Southern Continent, and another expedition was soon equipped to solve this dilemma. On July 13, 1772, this time with two ships, *Resolution* and *Adventure*, Cook sailed for the Cape of Good Hope and then voyaged east through fog and ice, sleet and snow, at around latitude 60° south. Turning north, the two ships met at a rendezvous in Dusky Sound, New Zealand. Cook was able to precisely locate destinations because he had been given the first accurate marine chronometer with which to find longitude. The following Antarctic summer, 1773–1774, Cook again sailed back into the ice and snow, reaching 71° south and finally proving that a habitable southern continent really did not exist.

PICKERSGILL HARBOR, DUSKY SOUND, NEW ZEALAND

Returning from Antarctic waters in March 1773, Cook moored the *Resolution* in a small creek "so near the shore as to reach it by a large tree which growed in a horizontal direction over the water so long that the top of it reached our gunwale." To the delight of the seamen, the creek had plentiful supplies of fresh water and fish. One sailor can be seen here returning from the astronomical observation tent that was set up onshore.

PICKING UP ICE

Voyaging through Antarctic waters, Cook's crews replenished their water supply by cutting ice from icebergs, which they called "ice islands." In the absence of land in these latitudes, they also shot sea birds to obtain fresh meat. William Hodges drew this scene in January 1773.

COOK'S CHRONOMETER

At his fourth attempt, John Harrison succeeded in making a practical and reliable marine chronometer. It was tested on a sea voyage in 1761 and over four weeks was out by only five seconds. However, Harrison was awarded only half the Board of Longitude's $30,000 prize, for the chronometer also had to be capable of precise reproduction. In 1772, Cook took with him this copy by Larcum Kendall, on trial. Its accuracy permitted Harrison to get the other half of the prize in 1773.

THE CAPE OF GOOD HOPE

Cook was accompanied on this voyage by 28-year-old artist William Hodges, who painted this view from the deck of the *Resolution* on its voyage south. The *Adventure* can be seen inshore, with her sails back and Cape Town, South Africa, behind. Hodges went on to paint many more dramatic landscapes on the voyage.

MAORI CLUB AX

Although generally friendly, the Maori people of New Zealand could be dangerous. In December 1773, Captain Tobias Furneaux of the *Adventure* missed a rendezvous with Cook's *Resolution*, so his ship was alone in Queen Charlotte Sound, New Zealand. The ship's cutter and ten men were sent to get provisions, but they were all killed—and some were eaten. In their attack, the Maori probably used a club ax of the type shown here.

TAHITIAN SWATTERS

This long-haired fly swatter—
"very ingeniously wrought"—
was obtained by trade by
Joseph Banks from an island
close to Tahiti; the flanking
figures are handles.

The Pacific Peoples
The Second Voyage, 1772–1775

During the Antarctic winters, Cook explored and charted many of the islands of the Pacific. Both in 1773 and 1774 he was welcomed back to Tahiti, where a favorite anchorage was Matavai Bay. In 1773, the crews of both *Resolution* and *Adventure* were sick with scurvy, and Cook spread a sail as an awning on the beach, where the sick could recover in comfort. The hills inland gave the artist of the voyage, William Hodges, a trained landscape painter, subject matter to his taste. The splendor of the scenes he painted did a great deal to make Europeans think the Pacific Islands were paradise. The Tahitians were depicted in noble, classical poses, but Cook suffered from their eagerness to acquire items from the ships, by theft if not trade. The women pursued this practice as much as the men.

Resolution *and* Adventure *in Matavai Bay, Tahiti, William Hodges, 1773*

OMAI

Omai was from Huahine, near Tahiti. Intelligent and friendly, he acted as an interpreter and wished to visit Great Britain. Captain Furneaux of the *Adventure* brought him back to London, where he became a celebrity before being returned to Tahiti in 1777.

BAKING BREADFRUIT

The breadfruit tree grows naturally in Tahiti. The Tahitians eat the fruit and are shown above cooking it. Joseph Banks proposed growing the fruit in the West Indies in order to feed plantation slaves. William Bligh, who accompanied Cook on his second voyage, delivered the trees in 1791, but the slaves shunned the fruit because of its bland taste.

TAHITIAN WAR GALLEYS

In Tahiti in 1774, Cook came across an assembled fleet of war canoes and galleys—more than 300 vessels—drawn up for inspection by the principal chief. They carried flags and streamers and "made a grand and noble appearance such as was never seen before in this sea." Cook watched as, lashed together in divisions, they practiced paddling furiously to land together on the beach, where they engaged in mock battle. After William Hodges drew them, Cook had the pleasure of going onboard several boats.

CAPTAIN JAMES COOK
-A Timeline-

~1771~

Endeavour *returns to England. Cook is chosen to command a second voyage.*

~1772–73~

Resolution *and* Adventure *search for the Great Southern Continent.*

~1773~

Resolution *circles the South Pacific, discovering the Tonga islands.*

~1773-74~

Cook reaches latitude 71° south, looking for the Great Southern Continent.

FOUR TONGAN WAR CLUBS

Although the Tongan people were friendly to Cook, their chieftains had to defend their islands. Because they traveled and fought from canoes, paddles sometimes served as war clubs. The clubs above are thought to have been collected by Cook, probably by trade—the Tongan people had an insatiable appetite for nails. Cook's voyages were the first to bring back collections of such ethnographic items, giving rise to the study of anthropology.

THE LANDING IN EROMANGA, NEW HEBRIDES

In August 1774, Cook landed to ask for wood and water but was met by a large group armed with clubs, darts, stones, bows, and arrows. He suspected the worst and stepped back into his boat, upon which the crowd surged forward, shooting and throwing missiles, and tried to drag the boat up the beach. Cook's musket misfired, and he had to order others to fire. Four men died, but Cook's boat escaped.

The Pacific Peoples
The Second Voyage, 1772–1775

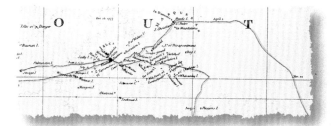

Exploring west of Tahiti in 1773, Cook discovered the Tonga islands, where the people were so kind that he called them the Friendly Islands. Farther east in 1774, he found Easter Island with its giant statues, and the Marquesas, islands known to the Spaniards but whose location had never been charted. Returning west again, he found New Hebrides (now Vanuatu), inhabited by Melanesians, who were less friendly than the Polynesians so far encountered. These island groups had a special beauty, with many unusual flowering trees and shrubs, including the breadfruit tree in Tahiti. However, drinking water was often scarce, while underwater coral reefs made navigation perilous. Cook's achievement was thus even greater, and he was honored on his return home.

THE MONUMENTS OF EASTER ISLAND

In March 1774, Cook sent 27 men to explore Easter Island. They found seven stone figures, four of which were still standing, with three overturned, perhaps by an earthquake. The figures represented men up to the waist, with large ears. They were around 18 ft. (5.5m) high and 5 ft. (1.5m) wide, "ill shaped," and had large "hats" of red rock on their heads, like some Egyptian gods. One hat measured more than 5 ft. (1.5m) in diameter. The figures appeared to mark burial places—among the stones were several human bones, as shown in Hodges' painting.

The Pacific Further Explored

The Third Voyage, 1776–1780

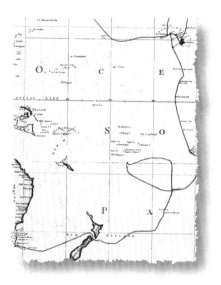

In July 1776, one year after returning home, Cook again sailed for the Pacific. This was partly to return Omai to Tahiti, partly because there was hope of finding a northwest passage from the Pacific to the Atlantic for trading purposes, and partly to examine some desolate islands discovered by the French—Britain's enemy—near the Cape of Good Hope. The *Resolution* and *Discovery*, his two ships, headed for Tasmania (then known as Van Diemen's Land) and New Zealand before sailing through the Tonga islands to Tahiti. Aiming for the west coast of Canada, Cook pressed north at the end of the year, spending Christmas 1777 on a coral atoll, Christmas Island, before discovering the Sandwich Islands, including Hawaii.

STONE TOOLS & TATTOOING INSTRUMENTS, TAHITI

The tools and instruments in use in the Pacific Islands were Stone Age in their sophistication. European society, which took the Bible literally, assumed that primitive societies were closer to nature and the innocence of the Garden of Eden. However, the Islanders' practice of human sacrifice, loose morals, and thefts from Cook's ships conflicted with Christian ideals and made Europeans question their own beliefs.

KENDALL'S THIRD MARINE CHRONOMETER

Cook continued to benefit from the rapid improvement of navigational equipment. In the *Discovery*, he took another chronometer made by Larcum Kendall, who had been requested by the Board of Longitude to attempt to improve upon his previous copies of John Harrison's prizewinning model. The new "watch machine" was simpler, and mass production would permit merchant shipping and traders to follow where Cook had been.

A HUMAN SACRIFICE IN TAHITI

At this, his fourth visit to Tahiti, Cook was honored by being taken to a human-sacrifice ceremony intended to assist the chief in a local war. He made careful observations. No women were present and Cook had to remove his hat. Drums were beaten and prayers were uttered. A man, bruised from being beaten to death, was tied to a pole. One of his eyes was ceremoniously eaten before he was buried; then a dog was sacrificed and presented to their *atua*, or god.

A NIGHT DANCE BY WOMEN IN TONGA, OR THE FRIENDLY ISLANDS

Making his third visit to the Friendly Islands, Cook was entertained as an honored guest. The Tongan men sat in a semicircle and began a song with a rhythm beaten out on hollow pieces of bamboo. Then younger women encircled the men, singing and dancing, their bodies shining in the torch light: "the most beautiful forms that imagination can conceive." Quickening songs interspersed with savage shouts made it an exhilarating performance.

CAPTAIN JAMES COOK
-A Timeline-

~1774~

A wider Pacific circle discovers Easter Island, the Marquesas, and New Hebrides (Vanuatu).

~1775~

Cook returns to England.

~1776~

Cook begins his third Pacific voyage and sails south in the Resolution, *in company with the* Discovery.

Great Britain's American colonies declare their independence.

THE NOOTKA SOUND PEOPLE

Large numbers of natives visited the ships daily, some clearly from a long distance away. On first appearance, they generally went through the same ceremony. They first paddled with all their strength around the ships; a chief, his face covered with a mask of either a human or an animal face, then stood up with a spear or rattle in his hand and shouted a greeting. Sometimes this was followed by a song in which they all joined in and made a "very agreeable harmony," upon which they came closer and began to trade.

POLAR BEAR

Cook's companions spotted a white bear in the Arctic. John Webber, an artist, was only 24 years old when they set out, but he was accomplished at rapidly drawing broad landscapes and natural objects with precise detail. Above, he caught the huge size and dangerous character of the animal.

REPAIRING THE SHIPS

The *Resolution*'s fore- and mizzenmasts had to be replaced, and the rigging of her mainmast had to be renewed. Sheer legs were thus set up on the *Resolution*'s deck to remove the defective masts. New masts were cut and fashioned onshore, where smiths forged new fittings on the beach.

SEA OTTER

The sea otter's lustrous skin was greatly prized. Russian traders had been busy buying its pelts from Inuit and Native Americans since 1741, when Vitus Bering discovered the strait that bears his name. The Chinese paid high prices for them. Cook's report of the trade prompted British merchants in China, then other Europeans and Americans, to mount trading ventures. Soon the North Pacific was alive with ships.

Northwest Canada & Alaska
The Third Voyage, 1776–1780

Off the Canadian coast early in 1778, Cook first found a safe bay, later called Nootka Sound (below middle-left), in which to repair the *Resolution* and *Discovery*. He then coasted north, entering every inlet in search of a northwest passage. Everywhere he landed, Cook met the native peoples who lived on these coasts. Rounding Alaska, he pressed through the Bering Strait dividing the continents of Asia and North America and, peering through persistent fog, entered the Arctic Sea. At 20° north, he met pack ice and, unwilling to let his ships get trapped, turned back. Planning to return the next summer, he then sailed for the Sandwich Islands, where Hawaii seemed to offer a welcoming winter resting place.

SURVEY WORK

As soon as the ships were moored, portable observatories were set up on an elevated rock in order for the astromoners to make their observations. The longitude of the cove was settled with the utmost care, for this position would become a bearing for further navigation. In front of the tents, surveying work began to chart and map the waters and terrain of the sound.

BEAVER BOWL, INLAID WITH SHELL

The natives brought fish, furs, weapons, whale bladders full of oil, and even human skulls to exchange for any sort of metal—knives, chisels, nails, buttons. They stole as well as traded, and even Cook's own gold watch was taken, though later it was recovered. The greatest desire of the seamen was sea-otter pelts. This wooden bowl, carved in the shape of a beaver, was probably obtained in Nootka Sound.

SHOOTING "SEA HORSES"

Penetrating through the Bering Strait in August 1778 in latitude 20° north, Cook met an ice field, inhabited by "sea horses," or walrus. To obtain fresh meat, boats were sent from both ships to kill 12 of the great beasts. Cook was delighted and, to ensure that the meat was eaten, stopped all normal rations except bread.

The Death of Cook

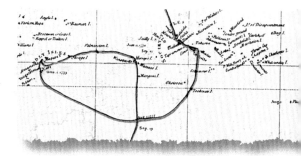

In Hawaii, Cook was greeted like a god. The Hawaiians were expecting their god Lono to arrive on a floating island with trees, not unlike the *Resolution*. Gifts and trade abounded, but so did thefts. Cook tried to punish the culprits and retrieve stolen equipment, sometimes by taking hostages. By February 1779, awe for Cook, and his own patience, had grown thin. While trying to retrieve a stolen ship's cutter, Cook was killed suddenly. Captain Charles Clerke of the *Discovery* finished looking for a northwest passage but was unsuccessful. Cook's voyages had nevertheless opened the largest ocean in the world to European trade and settlement. They had contributed to knowledge of different peoples and cultures, of Earth and its plants and animals, and of the planet's place in the universe. Moreover, they had been achieved with little loss of seamen's lives and much respect for other races. Cook set new standards for all explorers to follow.

HAWAIIAN SPEAR

The Hawaiians, like other Pacific Islanders, originally had only wood and stone weapons, against which they defended themselves with woven mats. These were no match for European firearms and swords made of metal. However, realizing the usefulness of metal, they traded and stole it whenever possible and made metal daggers. Cook was stabbed with one in the struggle before his death. Otherwise, the crowd by which he was overwhelmed was armed with spears and stones.

THE DEATH OF COOK

When the *Discovery's* cutter was taken on February 14, 1779, Cook went ashore to take the local chief hostage for its return. A hostile crowd gathered, which grew angrier when Cook himself fired at a man who threatened him, upon which the Hawaiians launched themselves at Cook's party. Cook was hit from behind with a club and then stabbed and drowned.

COOK'S SUCCESSOR IN THE PACIFIC

In 1789, William Bligh, the sailing master of the *Resolution* on the second voyage, suffered a mutiny after returning to Tahiti in the *Bounty* to collect breadfruit for the West Indies.

COOK UNDERMINED

Cook normally treated the Pacific Islanders with reasoned patience. In Hawaii, however, he started to act out of character and decided on a sudden descent on a Hawaiian village. He took armed marines and ordered their firearms to be loaded and fired to kill. It is now thought that stress and the poor diet of three long voyages, and possibly illness, had undermined his understanding and caution.

BRITISH PISTOL

This pistol was the sort issued to sea officers, and Cook would have carried one as required. When he was killed, he was carrying a two-barreled musket, one barrel loaded with "small shot," the other with ball. He was accompanied by a lieutenant and nine marines, all armed with muskets. The number of guns was intended to threaten. The disadvantage of these weapons in a crowd was that they could not be reloaded quickly.

CAPTAIN JAMES COOK
-A TIMELINE-

~1777~

Cook returns to New Zealand, Tonga, and Tahiti and discovers Christmas Island.

~1778~

After discovering Hawaii, Cook explores the northwest coast of North America and passes through the Bering Strait.

~1779~

Cook returns to Hawaii and is killed.

~1780~

On October 4, after exploring the northwest coast of the Pacific and again penetrating the Bering Strait in search of a northwest passage, Cook's ships return to England.

POEDUA—A HOSTAGE

In November 1777, two seamen deserted in the Society Islands, and to force the islanders to return them, Cook took hostage the 15-year-old daughter of the local chief, her brother, and her husband. Among friends, the three captives were not alarmed, but their father quickly secured the deserters. John Webber painted the girl's portrait (right).

The Elizabethan Explorers

The Age of Discovery by European explorers began in Portugal in 1415 with Prince Henry, otherwise known as Henry the Navigator. He sent ships out to explore the north and west coasts of Africa, bringing back riches such as ivory. Vasco da Gama (c. 1460–1524), also Portuguese, rounded the Cape of Good Hope, off the southernmost tip of Africa, and opened the first European maritime route to India. Later Portuguese explorers went on to discover routes to Japan, Southeast Asia, and South America, which soon made Portugal one of the wealthiest nations in Europe. Spain, and later England, emulated these first voyages in their thirst for gold and other riches, most of which (except in the Far East) were plundered from the native inhabitants of the countries they visited. Except for advances made in compiling more accurate navigational charts, very little scientific data was gathered on these early voyages, which were primarily motivated by money and trade.

ARAB INFLUENCE

Arab explorers from North Africa extended their empire as far as northern Spain from the 500s–1200s. They sailed the Mediterranean and the Indian Ocean in small boats called dhows. They also developed sophisticated astronomical equipment, such as this astrolabe, which greatly influenced European mariners.

JOHN CABOT (c. 1450–1499)

The quest for new trade routes in Tudor England began with King Henry VII. He considered sponsoring Christopher Columbus on his voyage of discovery to the New World but instead chose to finance an expedition by the Italian John Cabot, who tried to find a new route to China and the Spice Islands via the fabled Northwest Passage. He believed he had reached China when he struck land, but it was in fact the coast of Newfoundland. He is seen here departing from Bristol, England, in 1497.

CHURCH MISSIONARIES

Although the prime objective of the early explorers had been money, with no real interest in colonization, the church had different views. Within a few years of the first expeditions, Christian missions were established to convert the pagan natives. Many missionaries fell victim to the natives, like the Franciscan missionaries shown here being eaten by Native American cannibals.

VERAGVA PARS

THE SHIPWRIGHT'S SKILL

One of the reasons given for England's sea superiority over Spain was the design of her warships. Sir John Hawkins was responsible for introducing revolutionary new designs by Matthew Baker and Peter Pett, which completely transformed the English navy. The new ships were smaller and sleeker than the cumbersome Spanish galleons. They were low at the bow but high at the stern, which made them much more maneuverable.

CELESTIAL GLOBE

This Flemish celestial globe of c. 1537 shows the somewhat limited understanding of the constellations in the skies of the Southern Hemisphere in Tudor times. Information gathered from the around-the-world voyages of Ferdinand Magellan, Francis Drake, and Thomas Cavendish was added later, but this lack of knowledge made any voyage in the southern oceans especially hazardous.

ELIZABETHAN EXPLORERS
-A TIMELINE-

~1460~
Prince Henry the Navigator dies.

~c. 1460~
Vasco da Gama is born.

~1497~
Vasco da Gama sets sail for the Indies.

~1498~
Vasco da Gama arrives in India.

~1499~
Vasco da Gama returns to Portugal.

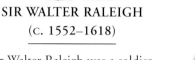

SIR WALTER RALEIGH
(c. 1552–1618)

Sir Walter Raleigh was a soldier, courtier, and explorer. He was an eager exponent of establishing English colonies in the New World, including Virginia, but they all failed. When James I acceded to the throne, he was accused of treason and imprisoned.

ELIZABETHAN EXPLORERS
-A Timeline-

~1502~
Vasco da Gama makes a second voyage to India to avenge the massacre of the Portuguese in Calicut.

~1562~
Sir John Hawkins makes his first successful slave-trading voyage to the West Indies.

~1565~
Tobacco is first introduced into England—probably by Hawkins.

NO SMOKE WITHOUT FIRE

While Raleigh is popularly credited with introducing potatoes and tobacco to England from the New World, that honor is now usually given to his contemporary Sir John Hawkins. Raleigh did make smoking fashionable at court, however, where he was one of Elizabeth I's favorites. Tobacco was usually smoked in long clay pipes, similar to those used by Native Americans. Raleigh is seen here (right) being doused with water by one of his servants, who feared he was on fire!

SIR JOHN HAWKINS (1532–1595)

Sir John Hawkins, a distant relative of Francis Drake, was responsible for modernizing Elizabeth's navy and played a major role in defeating the Spanish Armada. After the Armada, many of the crews were unpaid, and together with Drake, he set up a fund for distressed seamen called the Chatham Chest. He is said to have introduced the potato and tobacco into England. He died in 1595 during his and Drake's last ill-fated Caribbean voyage.

THE SEARCH FOR EL DORADO

In 1616, while still in prison, Raleigh persuaded James I to let him lead an expedition (his second) to the Orinoco River in Guiana to search for the fabled El Dorado (city of gold). The voyage failed, and Raleigh came home in disgrace. He was executed in 1618 under the original terms of his sentence.

The Elizabethan Explorers

The world in the 1400s was much more fragmented than it is today. Areas of advanced civilization existed in many places, including North Africa, the Mediterranean, China, and India, but each had only a limited knowledge of the existence of the others. Few Europeans at that time had any awareness of the world beyond Europe itself. Legends and travellers' tales abounded, so even those who did venture farther afield were seldom believed. The Atlantic Ocean was largely unexplored, and the existence of the Americas and the Pacific Ocean beyond had not been proved. Most of the world remained a mystery, uncharted and unmapped. For the brave adventurers setting out on their voyages of discovery with only limited navigational skills, it was a journey into the unknown, akin to today's space explorations of the Moon and beyond.

SIR RICHARD GRENVILLE (C. 1541–1591)

Sir Richard Grenville was another explorer who advocated the colonization of the New World rather than simply making piratic raids on Spanish treasure ships. He is best remembered for his gallant fight off Flores, in the Azores, in 1591. He was the commander of the *Revenge*, Francis Drake's former flagship against the Armada, and when he found himself surrounded by Spanish vessels, he insisted on continuing the fight alone. A harsh, arrogant man, he was fatally wounded and ordered the ship to be scuttled rather than given up to the Spanish, but his crew insisted on surrendering instead. Grenville died onboard the Spanish flagship shortly afterward.

SIR HUMPHREY GILBERT (C. 1539–1583)

Sir Humphrey Gilbert was another leading exponent of establishing English colonies in the New World. In 1578, he received "letters patent" from the queen, authorizing him to colonize new lands. Finally, in 1583, he gathered sufficient support and set off for Newfoundland. In Saint John's, already a flourishing port, he formally claimed the territory for England. He died on the way home, leaving his half brother, Walter Raleigh, to finish the task.

The Elizabethan Explorers

For modern observers of Elizabethan voyages of discovery, it is difficult to understand both the enormity of the enterprise and to perceive a pattern to the explorations. In truth, there never was a coherent plan. Since most European countries were at war with one another, each largely acted independently of the others. World exploration was thus little more than a race for riches stolen from primitive societies or to set up trade agreements with advanced communities.

England was still very much a lesser power in Europe, and ideas like scientific discovery, and even empire, came much later. Besides the obvious pillage, the spread of disease also became a major problem. Three hundred years on, we can still trace European influence across the globe, helping make the world a smaller, more unified place—though that could scarcely have been the intention of those original merchant adventurers who set out on their voyages into the unknown.

SIR MARTIN FROBISHER (C. 1535–1594)

In 1576, Martin Frobisher set out to discover the Northwest Passage and a trade route to China. He failed in this and two subsequent attempts, but he did make many important discoveries in the Arctic Ocean, including Baffin Island. Along with Drake and Hawkins, he was also a key figure in the defeat of the Spanish Armada in 1588. He died of gangrene from a bullet wound sustained when relieving the port of Brest, in northern France, from Spanish hands.

STRANGE SIGHTS

Explorers in the 1500s encountered strange sights on their intrepid voyages, including many alien cultures and plants and animals never before seen by Europeans. The women shown here (believed to come from Java, Indonesia) are killing themselves following the death of their king, an act witnessed by Thomas Cavendish on his circumnavigation (1586–1588).

MAP OF THE PIRATE SEAS

The first expeditions by English mariners were little more than acts of legalized piracy. Elizabeth I instructed her sea captains to intercept as many Spanish treasure ships as possible and steal their gold. Afterward, when the expeditions became more legitimate, the seas remained infested by pirates, opportunist cutthroats who attacked any ship and plundered its cargo.

ARMAMENTS

Most ships in the 1500s carried a small number of guns, similar to this bronze demicannon retrieved from the wreck of the *Mary Rose*, which sank in 1545. It was one of the first English warships to be equipped with gun ports cut into her sides. Cannon of this type were usually cast from iron or bronze and remained the principal form of armament on fighting ships for the next 300 years.

THOMAS CAVENDISH (1560–1592)

Shortly after Drake's return from his circumnavigation of the world, Thomas Cavendish was commissioned to emulate his epic voyage. He completed the trip in less time than Drake (1586–1588) but largely followed the same route. His was probably the first intentional voyage of circumnavigation. Both Magellan's and Drake's voyages appear to have had other motives, at least initially, and both were forced to complete their circumnavigation as the safest route home. In 1591, Cavendish set out again for the East Indies, but the voyage ended in disaster. Through the Strait of Magellan, the men killed penguins for sustenance, which putrefied, overtaking the ship with worms. Soon afterward, an especially nasty bout of scurvy broke out, killing around 75 percent of the crew.

ELIZABETHAN EXPLORERS
-A Timeline-

~1583~
Sir Humphrey Gilbert claims Newfoundland for England.

~1584~
Sir Walter Raleigh establishes the first colony in Virginia.

~1591~
Sir Richard Grenville of the Revenge dies after being outnumbered by a Spanish fleet in the Azores.

~1595~
Sir John Hawkins dies.

~1616~
Raleigh sets out to discover El Dorado but fails and returns to England in disgrace.

~1618~
Sir Walter Raleigh is executed for treason.

PORTUGUESE EXPLORERS
-A Timeline-

~1488~
The Cape of Good Hope is reached by Bartolomeu Dias.

~1494~
The Treaty of Tordesillas between Spain and Portugal is signed, dividing the non-Christian world between them.

~1500~
Brazil is discovered by Pedro Álvares Cabral.

~1524~
Vasco da Gama is appointed viceroy of India.

Vasco da Gama dies and is buried in Cochin (Kochi), India.

~1530~
The Portuguese establish trading bases in Bombay (Mumbai), India, and Sri Lanka.

THE RICHES OF THE INDIES

Bartolomeu Dias was given the task of preparing da Gama's ships for the voyage. He loaded them with objects to trade with the Africans such as hawk bells, rings, cloth, and olive oil. It did not occur to him that the rulers of the Indies would not be impressed with these objects. This picture shows how wealthy and abundant in food the Indies were. This cargo caused da Gama problems when he arrived in India.

DA GAMA'S SHIPS

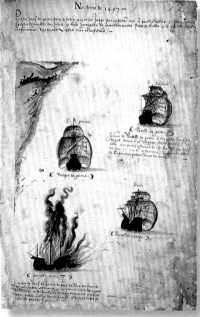

Da Gama had a fleet of four ships: the *Saõ Gabriel,* the *Saõ Rafael,* the *Berrio,* and a storage ship that had no name but carried three years' supply of food and drink. The ships set off from Lisbon on July 8, 1497. This picture (left) shows the store ship burning. This was deliberately done by da Gama because he was afraid that if the store ship was lost in bad weather, his crew would starve. The supplies were crammed onto the other ships before the empty store ship was set on fire.

CLAIMING LAND FOR PORTUGAL

Among the supplies that da Gama and his crew carried on his voyage were stone crosses called *padrões.* These were set in high ground to act as markers for crews to follow. They were also used when Portugal claimed any newly discovered land. This cross is in Malindi in modern-day Kenya. Da Gama had a difficult time in East Africa because Arab traders did not welcome them there.

India & the Indian Ocean

The Portuguese did more than build forts to protect their trade routes to the Indies. In 1494, Spain and Portugal signed the Treaty of Tordesillas, which divided the world between the two countries. It gave Spain control over all non-Christian lands west of an imaginary line in the mid-Atlantic. Portugal was given everything to the east. This meant that only the Portuguese could use the route around Africa to Asia. It took ten years after Bartolomeu Dias had discovered the way around Africa for Portuguese ships to finally reach India. The new king of Portugal, Manuel I, chose Vasco da Gama to lead this expedition.

da Gama ———— Cabral ————

VASCO DA GAMA
(c. 1460–1524)

Very little is known about Vasco da Gama's early life. He was born sometime in the early 1460s and became a soldier. He also studied navigation from Portuguese sailors. It was this skill, together with his military knowledge and qualities as a leader, that made him the ideal candidate for Portugal's first expedition to the Indies.

DEALING WITH MUTINY

King Manuel I chose da Gama because he had a reputation for being a good leader and for maintaining discipline. At first, da Gama had to sail out into the Atlantic to catch the wind that would take him eastward. He was out of sight of land for 13 weeks. Some of the crew thought they would never see land again. They mutinied and tried to force da Gama to return home, but he convinced them that they would land soon. The ringleaders of the mutiny were arrested and bound in chains.

India & the Indian Ocean

When da Gama reached the East African port of Malindi, he saw four ships that looked strange to him. This was his first contact with Indian traders. The sultan of Malindi turned out to be friendly and helped da Gama with the rest of his trip. When da Gama set off across the Indian Ocean, he brought a pilot named Ahmed bin Majid. With his help, da Gama managed to sail across the Indian Ocean in only 23 days. He arrived in Calicut, the main trading city in southern India, on May 20, 1498. The eastward route to Asia had been found.

BOMBARDING CALICUT

Another explorer named Pedro Álvares Cabral was sent to Calicut after da Gama had returned to Portugal. He set up a trading center in Calicut, left behind some Portuguese traders, and sailed home. Local Muslims attacked the center and killed everybody inside. Da Gama was sent to take revenge. When he reached Calicut in 1502, he bombarded the city with cannon. From then on, the Portuguese controlled the Indian trade routes using military force.

HINDUS OR CHRISTIANS?

Until da Gama reached India, no European had even heard of Hinduism, the main religion of India. When da Gama first saw a Hindu temple, he was convinced that the people must be Christians. He thought a statue of a goddess, like the one shown on the left, was the Virgin Mary. Images of gods and goddesses painted on the walls seemed to be Christian saints. Da Gama returned to Portugal with tales of Indian Christians.

RETURN TO PORTUGAL

The picture (left) shows the king of Portugal, Manuel I, greeting da Gama on his return from India.

Da Gama had set off from Calicut on August 29, 1498. He decided to avoid East Africa. Such a long voyage without taking on fresh supplies took a terrible toll on the crew. When da Gama reached Lisbon in September 1499, only 54 out of the original crew of 170 were still alive. But King Manuel was overjoyed. Portugal had beaten Spain in the race to reach the Indies.

BUILDING AN EMPIRE

From centers such as Goa and the rebuilt city of Calicut, shown here, the Portuguese began to take control of the rest of the Asian trade routes. They reached China in 1513 and Japan in 1542. The Portuguese knew that many of the spices they found in India came from islands in Southeast Asia. They decided that they had to control the route to these islands. In 1511, Afonso de Albuquerque captured the Muslim port of Malacca, which controlled this route. From Malacca, the Portuguese could easily reach the islands that grew spices.

FIGHTING FOR CONTROL

The Portuguese were determined to take control of trade with India. King Manuel sent two commanders, Afonso de Albuquerque and Francisco de Almeida, to carry out this task. De Almeida sailed along the East African coast and attacked the Arab traders who had caused da Gama such difficulties. Muslim oared galleys were no match for Portuguese ships, and in the Battle of Diu, the entire Muslim fleet was destroyed. Goa was captured by Afonso de Albuquerque in 1510. He burned the city to the ground and built a new city. This picture shows a Portuguese-style building in Goa.

ARRIVAL IN CALICUT

The ruler of Calicut was named Zamorin. When da Gama met Zamorin, he laid out the gifts that he had brought with him. Zamorin was insulted by what he saw as cheap goods and sent da Gama away. Da Gama was allowed to trade but could not compete with the Arab traders. He spent three months in Calicut but managed to buy only a few spices. After a dispute with Zamorin over taxes, da Gama decided to sail home.

Renaissance & Other Explorers

AMERIGO VESPUCCI (1451–1512)

Vespucci was an Italian sailor who had a continent named after him. He claimed to have made four voyages to the New World, but only two are certain. His travel writings were very popular, and a German mapmaker named the New World map he was making "Amerigo," or America.

The exploration of the Americas and Asia continued long after they were first encounted by Europeans. The explorers who came after Columbus and da Gama had many reasons for exploring these newfound lands. Sometimes, it was simply a love of adventure and danger. Many of them, however, hoped to find land and wealth and make themselves and their monarchs rich. Others went with a missionary zeal, wanting to convert anyone they met to Christianity. Most of the explorers of North America and Canada were either English or French. The exploration of South America and the Indies was left to the Spanish and Portuguese.

WILLIAM DAMPIER (1651–1715)

Dampier was born in England in 1651. His early life at sea included a trip to Newfoundland in Canada. In 1698, he led a scientific expedition to lands to the south of Asia that had just been discovered. His voyage took him to the west coast of Australia and the islands of Indonesia.

HENRY HUDSON (1565–1611)

Hudson tried to find the Northeast and Northwest passages. His first voyage was in 1607, when he tried to find the Northeast Passage, but his ship was blocked by ice. During his fourth voyage in 1610 to find the Northwest Passage, he was forced to spend the winter in freezing conditions in a bay now named after him. The crew mutinied and set him adrift in a small boat. He was never heard from again.

THOMAS CAVENDISH

Thomas Cavendish was an English explorer and the third person to sail around the globe. He set off in July 1586 from Plymouth with three ships. He discovered Port Desire in Argentina before sailing through the Strait of Magellan. He attacked Spanish ships and settlements and then sailed across the Pacific, returning to England in 1588. He died while sailing to China.

Animum fortuna sequatur

~1551~
English merchants form a company to fund an expedition to find the Northeast Passage.

~1553~
Sir Hugh Willoughby and Richard Chancellor set off from London to find the Northeast Passage.

Willoughby dies and Chancellor meets Ivan the Terrible.

~1554~
Richard Chancellor reaches Moscow and establishes trade relations with Russia.

~1563~
Juan Fernández sails from Callao, Peru, to Valparaiso, Chile.

~1586~
Thomas Cavendish sets out on an attempt to sail around the globe.

~1609~
Henry Hudson makes his first expedition to North America.

JUAN FERNÁNDEZ
(1536–1604)

Juan Fernández was a Spanish navigator and explorer. In 1563, he sailed from Callao, Peru, to Valparaiso, Chile, which was considered a daring feat. He went on to discover several Pacific islands in 1574. There is some evidence that he reached Australia and New Zealand in 1576.

SAMUEL DE CHAMPLAIN (1575–1635)

Samuel de Champlain was the son of a French naval captain. He traveled to North America and Canada 12 times between 1603–1616. From 1604–1607, he mapped most of the Canadian Atlantic coast. In 1608, he founded the tiny settlement of Quebec, which went on to become the capital of French colonists in Canada. He discovered the Ottawa River and Lakes Champlain, Ontario, and Huron.

Hernando Cortés & the Aztecs

The Spanish conquered Cuba in 1511 under the command of Diego Velázquez de Cuéllan. From there, they set out in ships to search for gold on the Central American mainland. In 1517, Francisco de Córdoba sailed to the Yucatán Peninsula, on the Mexican mainland, where he met the Maya people, but they quickly drove him away. Another expedition one year later was more successful, and they brought back gold to Cuba. In 1519, Velázquez ordered Hernando Cortés, who had helped in the conquest of Cuba, to lead an expedition to explore the interior of Mexico. An argument between the two men led to Cortés renouncing Velázquez and Cortés setting off with his own private army. Little did Cortés realize that he would encounter a great empire, one of the largest cities in the known world, and that with only a few hundred soldiers, he would destroy both.

HERNANDO CORTÉS

Hernando Cortés was born in 1485 into a Spanish noble family. He studied for two years at the University of Salamanca. In 1504, he arrived in the New World, and he fought in the conquest of Cuba in 1511.

MARINA THE TRANSLATOR

Soon after he landed in the Yucatán, Cortés was given slaves as a gift by the local people. One of these was a woman whom the Spaniards called Marina. Her knowledge of the area and her ability to speak both the local Maya language and Nahuatl, the Aztec language, made her invaluable to Cortés. However, he still needed a Spaniard who could speak Mayan in order to talk to the Aztecs.

MOUNT POPOCATÉPETL

On their way to the Aztec capital, the Spaniards passed the volcano Mount Popocatépetl. It was belching smoke. They had never seen a live volcano before, and Cortés sent some men up the mountain to see where the smoke was coming from. They were forced back by the hot ash.

FIRST MEETING

This picture shows the first meeting between Montezuma, the Aztec ruler, and Cortés. When Cortés and his men reached the Aztec capital, Montezuma was there to welcome him. He stood under a canopy of feathers, gold, silver, and jewels, and he wore magnificent clothes, including shoes with golden soles. He received Cortés and his men with honor and allowed them to enter Tenochtitlán, the Aztec capital.

WERE THE SPANIARDS GODS?

Cortés had only 600 soldiers and could easily have been defeated by the Aztec soldiers before they reached the capital. But Montezuma held back. It was a special year in the Aztec calendar, when Quetzalcoatl, one of their gods, might return to the Aztecs and destroy them. It was said that this god would be tall with white skin, a beard, and long dark hair. Cortés closely fitted this description. Montezuma had to decide whether the Spaniards were men or gods. He decided that Cortés was the god he was told would return, and he prepared to welcome him.

THE AZTECS SEE THE SPANISH

Montezuma heard about the Spaniards and sent messengers to meet them and report back. The messengers' report showed that the Spaniards, and their horses, looked very strange to them.
"They dress in metal and wear metal hats on their heads. Their deer carry them on their backs wherever they wish to go. These deer are as tall as the roof of a house."

THE GREAT TEMPLE

At the very center of Tenochtitlán was the Great Temple, a single pyramid with two shrines. One was dedicated to Huitzilopochtli, the god of war, the other to Tlaloc, the rain god. This cutaway shows that several temples had been built on this site and that the Aztecs built each new temple over the old one.

THE WALLED PRECINCT

This model shows the complex of buildings that was isolated from the rest of Tenochtitlán. Alongside the huge temples were houses for the priests and recreation areas.

INSIDE THE TEMPLE

At the center of the Great Temple was the oldest inner temple. It was there that human sacrifices often took place.

COATEPANTLI

The wall round the complex was called the Coatepantli. It is believed that the wall was around 10 ft. (3m) high, and each side measured around 1,300 ft. (400m). There were probably four gates that led into the area.

TEMPLE OF QUETZALCOATL

This circular temple was dedicated to Quetzalcoatl, the god of knowledge. The conical roof may have been made of straw.

AZTEC PYRAMIDS

Aztecs built their temples at the top of very high pyramids. The temples were used for religious ceremonies and sacrifices. The sacrifices would take place at the entrances, after which the blood and limbs of the victims were swept down the steps.

The Aztec Empire

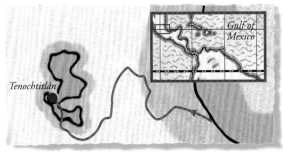

Cortés's journey to Tenochtitlán, 1519

When Cortés and his men arrived in Tenochtitlán they had reached the center of a huge empire that stretched from the Atlantic to the Pacific coast. The Aztecs were a wandering tribe until they began to build the city of Tenochtitlán around a temple to one of their gods, Huitzilopochtli, in around the year 1300. They built the city on a series of islands on Lake Texcoco. The city had aqueducts, canals, and a huge causeway linking it to the mainland. By the 1500s, it had a population of around 300,000 and was larger than any European city. The wealth of the Aztecs came from conquered peoples who were forced to pay tribute to them.

TLACHTLI

This was the first building seen after entering the west gate. It was used to play a ball game called tlachtli. Played by ruling families, it involved hitting a rubber ball through a hoop using the shoulders or hips.

SACRIFICE

The Aztecs believed that their gods needed to be fed with blood in order to survive. If the gods died, the world would come to an end. Sacrificial victims were first stretched over a stone by four priests. The flint knife attached to this ornate hilt would have been used by a fifth priest to cut open the victim's chest, and his still-beating heart would have been removed and placed in a bowl. The arms and legs of the victim were eaten. Most of the victims were prisoners captured in battles.

The Aztec Empire

As the Spanish advanced through the Aztec empire and entered Tenochtitlán, they encountered a civilization that must have seemed very cruel and yet very advanced. The Aztecs had a huge and fantastically wealthy empire of at least 12 million people, advanced agriculture, a magnificent city with beautiful palaces, a zoo, and colorful gardens. They were the most powerful people in Central America. One of Cortés's soldiers, Bernal Díaz del Castillo, later wrote of his encounter with the Aztecs, *"With such wonderful sights to gaze on we did not know what to say, or if what we saw was real."* Their calendars, ways of writing, and the gods they worshiped may have sounded strange to the Spaniards, but Aztec life was as sophisticated as anything that would have been found in other parts of the known world.

A MULTITUDE OF GODS

The Aztecs believed in many gods and goddesses. Each of them looked after an aspect of Aztec life. There were four important gods. Tlaloc was the god of rain and storms. Tezcatlipoca was the god of darkness and evil. Huitzilopochtli was the god of light and war. Quetzalcoatl was the god of life. The Aztec priests were very powerful people.

POLE CEREMONY

Aztec religion demanded many different ceremonies and rituals. In one of them, men would use feathers to dress themselves as birds and would then be attached to ropes and swung around in a wide circle. As this photograph shows, this practice is still continued in modern Mexico.

PLAYING PATOLLI

Along with ball games such as tlachtli, the Aztecs also played board games like patolli. The board was divided into four sections and totaled 52 squares, symbolizing the 52 years of the Aztec century. The game involved throwing dice and different-colored beans until one player got three beans in a row. This and other games were often of religious significance and could have dire consequences—the loser and his family could become slaves. In tlachtli, players were often badly injured, and the loser might be sacrificed.

AZTEC CALENDAR STONE

This large stone, one of the largest Aztec sculptures found, shows their belief that the world has been through four stages that have been created and destroyed. The Aztecs believed they were living in the fifth age, which would be destroyed by a massive earthquake. The human race and the Sun and the Moon were created at the start of the fifth world. In the center of the stone is the face of the Sun.

READING AND WRITING

The Aztecs did not use letters for writing words. They had a type of picture-writing system using symbols called glyphs (an example is shown left) where every object was represented as a drawing. There were strict rules about how these drawings were created. Aztec books were called codices. They were made out of bark, and the pages were joined together to make one long book.

COAST NEAR CEMPOALA

The Aztecs were wealthy because the people they conquered had to pay tribute to them. When the Aztecs took over new lands, they allowed the people living there to continue following their own lives as long as they sent a tribute every year. This tribute was usually locally produced food. On the coast of Cempoala, this would have been fish.

THE DEATH OF MONTEZUMA

When Cortés first left the city, fighting had broken out between the Aztecs and the Spanish. The Aztec leaders decided to depose the imprisoned Montezuma and replace him with his brother Cuitláhuac. Cortés did not realize that Montezuma was no longer seen as the ruler of the Aztecs, and he brought him to the roof of the royal palace to appeal to his people, but they replied by throwing stones at him and attacking the palace. One of the stones hit Montezuma, and he was later found dead. Both sides accused the other of killing him. His body was taken away and thrown into one of the nearby canals.

HERNANDO CORTÉS & THE AZTECS
-A Timeline-

~1485~
Hernando Cortés is born.

~1504~
Cortés sails for Hispaniola.

~1519~
Cortés and his army enter Tenochtitlán.

~1520~
The Aztecs drive Cortés out of Tenochtitlán.

~1521~
Fighting between the Aztecs and Spaniards starts.

Cortés returns to Tenochtitlán with a new army, and the Aztecs finally surrender.

~1547~
Cortés dies near Seville, Spain.

THE SIEGE BEGINS

Along with his new army, Cortés also had built 12 or 13 ships that he armed with cannon from Cuba. He used these on the lake that surrounded the island city of Tenochtitlán to bombard the Aztec defenders. The Aztecs found themselves attacked from both inside and outside their city. Starving and weak with disease, the Aztecs held out against the Spanish and their allies for several months.

SMALLPOX IN THE CITY

In the end, it was not Spanish weapons that defeated the Aztecs. An outbreak of smallpox, a disease brought over from Europe, spread throughout the city, and many people died even before the siege began.

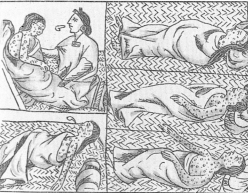

The Destruction of the Aztec Empire

After several days in Tenochtitlán, Cortés and his small army began to worry for their safety. They had seen the bloodstained steps of the Aztec temples and thought that the Aztecs were devil worshipers. They felt that it was only Montezuma who stopped the Aztecs from killing them all. Cortés decided to take Montezuma prisoner and to use him to rule the Aztecs. By then, Montezuma must have realized that these men were not gods. Cortés stayed for several months before leaving to deal with a rival expedition from Cuba.

THE EMPIRE DESTROYED

Cuauhtémoc, a nephew of Montezuma, became the new Aztec ruler and had to face Cortés's attack. He held out for four months, fighting on the streets of Tenochtitlán, before finally surrendering in August 1521. He was tortured and hanged.

AZTEC GOLD

The Aztecs believed they could appease the Spanish by giving them vast amounts of gold. Montezuma took them to the treasure house, where, according to one Aztec, *"The Spaniards stripped the feathers from the golden shields. They put all the gold in one large pile and set fire to everything else, even if it was valuable. They then melted the gold and turned it into bars."*

CORTÉS RETURNS

It was while Cortés was away that the Spaniards attacked the Aztecs. Cortés returned and tried to use Montezuma to calm the Aztecs, but the royal palace was besieged, and he had to fight his way out of Tenochtitlán. In May 1521, he came back with an army of 100,000 local people who hated the Aztecs. He cut off all supplies of food and water to the city before launching his final attack.

ATHABALIBA
ultimus Rex Peruanorum

The Destruction of the Inca Empire

The Spaniards in Central America heard rumors of a land in the south called Biru, or Peru, that was filled with gold and other precious metals. Francisco Pizarro decided to sail down the coast from Panama City, which the Spaniards had built in 1519. He led an expedition in 1527 and discovered the city of Túmbez. They were welcomed by the inhabitants and shown a great deal of gold and silver. Pizarro was now convinced that he had found a huge source of gold, and he returned to Spain. King Charles V gave him permission to conquer this new land and made him governor and captain-general of Peru. Pizarro returned in 1530 with an army of around 180 soldiers.

CIVIL WAR

Pizarro was helped by the fact that the Inca were fighting a civil war. An Incan ruler was called the Sapa Inca. In 1527, the Sapa Inca, Huayna Capac, died of smallpox. He had two sons, Huascar and Atahualpa, who both claimed his title. The final battle was fought as Pizarro approached and Huascar had been taken prisoner.

DEMAND FOR GOLD

After he was taken prisoner himself, Atahualpa thought that if he gave the Spaniards enough gold to fill a large room, they would let him go. Pizarro agreed to release him, and Atahualpa ordered gold to be stripped from temples and palaces. More than seven tons of gold were collected and melted down.

FRANCISCO PIZARRO (c.1471–1541)

Unlike many Spanish explorers, Pizarro was not born into a noble family. He was uneducated and could not read or write. He worked on a farm before coming to Central America to seek his fortune. He was killed during a power struggle in Lima, Peru, in 1541.

THE END OF THE INCA

With the death of Atahualpa, Incan resistance subsided. The Spaniards entered Cuzco on November 15, 1533. In 1536, Manco Inca, a puppet ruler, rose against the Spanish and almost succeeded in driving them out. It took another 36 years to finally subdue the whole Inca empire.

ATAHUALPA EXECUTED

Atahualpa had already been deceived once, and now Pizarro was ready to deceive him again, since he did not intend to release him. Pizarro wanted more than gold. He also planned to rule the Inca. On July 16, 1533, he had Atahualpa strangled with a piece of rope. Atahualpa was baptized just before his death so that his soul was "saved." His sisters asked to be buried alive with him, but the shocked Spaniards, who attended the funeral, refused.

FRANCISCO PIZARRO & THE INCA
-A Timeline-

~1502~
Francisco Pizarro sails for Hispaniola.

~1532~
Atahualpa is seized by Pizarro.

~1533~
Atahualpa is executed and Cuzco is finally taken.

~1535~
Lima, Peru, is founded by Pizarro.

~1541~
Pizarro is killed.

PIZARRO AND ATAHUALPA MEET

Atahualpa was confident after defeating his brother, and he was curious to meet Pizarro. Although he took 3,000 soldiers with him to the meeting, he agreed that they would be unarmed after Pizarro said that he would not be harmed. The Spanish soldiers, although they were vastly outnumbered, brought their muskets and cannon with them. When Atahualpa was captured, hundreds of his soldiers were killed trying to defend him with no weapons.

Other Explorers of South America

PEDRO DE ALVARADO

Alvarado was second in command to Cortés during the conquest of the Aztecs. After Tenochtitlán was destroyed and Mexico City built, he became its first mayor. In 1523, he conquered and settled Guatemala, and he later assisted in the conquest of Honduras.

Although the Spanish explorers had a reputation for being bloodthirsty and cruel, it must be remembered that they conquered the great civilizations of the Aztecs and Inca with only a few hundred soldiers. This must have taken a lot of courage and daring, and a certain amount of good luck. Pizarro and Cortés were not the only explorers of South and Central America. Many more men set out into unexplored areas with little idea of the dangers that lay ahead of them.

JUAN PONCE DE LEÓN

De León was born in 1460 and sailed with Columbus in 1493. He spent most of his time either in Cuba or fighting in Porto Rico. While he was in Cuba, he heard rumors of an island that had the fabled Fountain of Youth. He set sail to find the fountain, but instead he landed in Florida, his most famous discovery.

PEDRARIAS DÁVILA

Dávila established Spanish colonies in Panama in 1514 and Nicaragua in 1524. He also founded Panama City in 1519. It was Dávila who first sent Pizarro to conquer the Inca. He became governor of Nicaragua in 1526, where he stayed until his death in 1531.

PEDRO ÁLVARES CABRAL

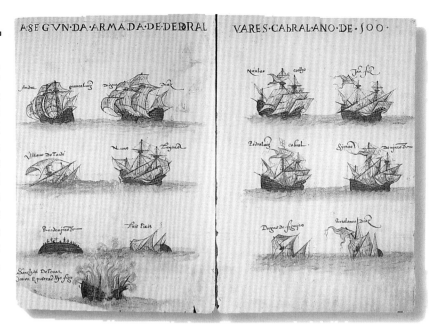

Cabral discovered Brazil almost by accident. In 1500, he had been sent by the king of Portugal to sail to India along the African coast. Soon after he set off, he was blown too far west and reached land that he named the Island of the True Cross. It was later named Brazil. He then set sail for India but on the way lost five of the 13 ships pictured here.

VASCO NÚÑEZ DE BALBOA

Balboa was an adventurer who stowed away on a ship from Hispaniola in the Caribbean to San Sebastián in Central America. He convinced the people there to resettle and then made himself their leader. He heard rumors of a huge sea and set off across Panama, with only a few hundred men, to find it. He was the first European to see the Pacific Ocean, which he claimed for Spain.

HERNANDO DE ALARCÓN

In 1540, Alarcón commanded two ships that supported an overland expedition from Mexico into the region now known as the southwestern United States. Alarcón sailed to the head of the Gulf of California and proved that there was no water passage between the gulf and the Pacific Ocean. He was also one of the first Europeans to sail along the Colorado River.

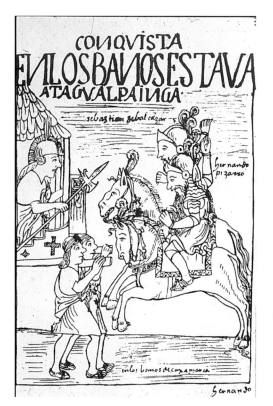

SEBASTIÁN DE BELALCÁZAR

Belalcázar served under Pedrarias Dávila during his campaign in Nicaragua in 1524. He then joined Pizarro on his expedition to Peru in 1531. In 1533, he set out on his own voyage and conquered the Inca in Ecuador.

PÁNFILO DE NARVÁEZ

Under the command of Diego de Velázquez, Narváez played an important part in the conquest of Cuba in 1511. In 1520 , he was sent to Mexico to arrest Cortés for treason. Cortés took him prisoner and released him one year later. In 1527, he led a two-year expedition to Florida. Narváez drowned, and only four of his men returned to Mexico.

ÁLVAR NUÑEZ CABEZA DE VACA

De Vaca joined the expedition to Florida under the leadership of Pánfilo de Narváez. The expedition was a disaster, and De Vaca was the only officer to survive. He and three other men eventually got back to Mexico. He was appointed the governor of the South American province of Río de la Plata—what is now Paraguay. In 1541, he led an expedition from Santos in Brazil to Asunción in Paraguay, a trip of more than 1,000 mi. (1,600km).

HERNANDO DE SOTO

De Soto is best known as the discoverer of the Mississippi River. He fought with Pizarro in the conquest of the Inca and was the first European to meet the Incan ruler Atahualpa. With the backing of the Spanish king, he led an expedition to Florida in 1539. He traveled through Florida, North and South Carolina, Alabama, and Mississippi. He discovered the Mississippi River in 1541.

Other Explorers of South America

Explorers went to South America for many reasons. The stories of the vast wealth of South and Central America that found their way back to Spain must have persuaded many to try to make their fortunes in these newly discovered lands. This is one of the reasons why the Spaniards treated their new subjects so cruelly. Although the Spanish king and some priests tried to protect the people from being mistreated, they had little effect. Many of these explorers were interested only in getting rich as soon as possible, and they were not concerned about those they had conquered. However, there were some who were driven by the belief that they were working for the glory of their god and country.

FRANCISCO DE ORELLANA

Orellana was the first person to explore the Amazon River. During an expedition into the interior of South America, Orellana found the Amazon and sailed along it for eight months until he reached the Atlantic Ocean. He then continued to Spain.

BERNAL DÍAZ DEL CASTILLO

Del Castillo was a Spanish soldier who kept a record of the conquest of the Aztecs by Cortés. Before joining Cortés, he had visited Panama and went to Yucatán in 1517 and 1518. In 1519, he accompanied Cortés to Mexico, and he claimed to have fought in more than 100 battles. He also fought in the conquest of El Salvador and Guatemala.

GONZALO JIMÉNEZ DE QUESADA

De Quesada was the Spanish conqueror of the Chibcha civilization of Columbia. In 1536, he set off to search for the legendary city of El Dorado. In 1537, he conquered the Chibcha and called the territory New Granada. While there, he founded the city of Bogotá, now the capital of Colombia.

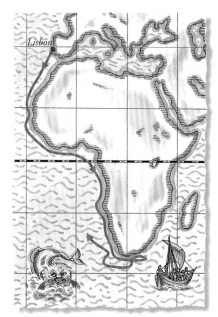

Lisbon

Diaz ━━━

The Exploration of Africa

Portugal and Spain had been conquered by the Moors in the 600s. Portugal finally threw out the Islamic invaders in 1249, and King John I of Portugal went on to conquer part of Morocco. Portugal's position on the Atlantic coastline made it ideally placed for overseas exploration, and Portuguese mariners began to look for a way to the Indies around Africa. By 1419, they had reached Madeira, and in 1431 they sailed to the Azores. In 1445, Portuguese sailors had gone around Cape Verde, the western tip of West Africa. By 1482, they crossed the equator and had reached the mouth of the Congo River.

ENCOUNTERS WITH AFRICANS

When the Portuguese sailors came into contact with the peoples who lived in Africa, they must have been amazed by their culture and appearance. Sculptures, such as this brass figure made by a member of the Ashanti people from modern-day Ghana, would have looked very strange. The Africans must also have been astonished by the Portuguese sailors when they first appeared off the coast in their tall ships.

PRINCE HENRY THE NAVIGATOR

Prince Henry the Navigator was the third son of John I. He spent his life studying navigation and directed the Portuguese exploration of the West African coast. He was a devout Christian who wanted to launch a crusade to drive the Muslims out of North Africa. Finding a way to Asia would help pay for this crusade and at the same time would weaken the hold that the Muslims had over the trade in gold and spices between Europe and Asia.

THE LEGEND OF PRESTER JOHN

One of the ways that Henry the Navigator hoped to destroy Muslim North Africa was to find Prester John. From the crusades onward, there were stories in Europe of a legendary Christian king named Prester John who ruled a kingdom somewhere in Africa. There were other stories that placed his kingdom in South Asia.

EAST AFRICAN STATES

The Portuguese who reached the East African coast found a world completely different from West Africa. The people of East Africa worshiped their own gods and had little contact with other cultures until the arrival of the Portuguese. East Africa was an important trading center for Arab sailors from the East. The Arabs built many ports and important buildings, such as this palace in Ethiopia (right). By the end of the 1500s, many of them had been taken over by the Portuguese.

WEST AFRICAN STATES

As the Portuguese explorers ventured farther down the West African coast, they found that many of the peoples they met belonged to large and powerful states. Little is known about these peoples since none of them had a written language. However, we know about their histories because they remembered past events in stories. Objects, such as these passport masks from the Dan people who lived in what is now Liberia, can also tell us a lot about the lives of the Africans who met the Portuguese explorers. Towns and cities such as Djenné and Gao were developed on the Niger River. These towns became part of the mighty Mali empire that stretched far into the interior of Africa. By the end of the 1400s, the Mali empire was itself taken over by the Songhai empire. These empires were of little interest to the Portuguese. There were other African states that the Portuguese traded with on a much more regular basis. These included the state of Akan, which was in modern-day Ghana, and the people of the Benin, in what is now Nigeria.

The Exploration of Africa

BARTOLOMEU DIAS

Dias's ships were driven out of sight of land by a fierce storm. When it became calm, he sailed north and found that the coast was now on his left and not his right as expected. He had sailed around the southern tip of Africa by accident.

The Portuguese were not interested in exploring the interior of Africa. They did trade with the peoples they encountered, but they were looking for a sea route to the Indies. However, they knew that places on the coast of Africa were important landing areas for ships. The route around Africa to Asia took many years to discover. In 1482, King John II sent Diogo Cão to find the Indies. Cão did not find it, but he did discover that Africa was much larger than many people thought. It was Bartolomeu Dias, in 1488, who finally sailed around the southern tip of Africa. He followed the coast of Africa and sailed farther south than any other European had gone until then.

CONSTRUCTION IN AFRICA

The Portuguese did not explore the interior of Africa, and they decided not to establish any African colonies at this stage. However, they knew they had to protect their trade routes to Asia, so they built a series of forts along the coastline. These would supply and protect Portuguese ships and keep out foreign competitors.

TRADING WITH AFRICANS

The two things that the Portuguese wanted when trading with the Akan and Benin peoples were gold and slaves. The Akan supplied most of West Africa's gold, which came from rivers in the interior of Africa. The Portuguese bought this gold from the Akan with slaves they had either captured themselves or bought from the Benin people. Many slaves were also transported back to Portugal and sold again.

THE CAPE OF GOOD HOPE

When Bartolomeu Dias reached the southern tip of Africa, he decided to call it *Cabo Tormentoso*, which means the "Cape of Storms." King John II rejected this name because it was too gloomy and gave it the name Cape of Good Hope—it raised hopes of eventually reaching the Indies.

JOHN CABOT

King Henry VII of England heard of Columbus's discoveries and approached John Cabot, who claimed that he could reach Asia across the North Atlantic. On his first voyage in 1497, he reached Canada and returned to a hero's welcome. However, Cabot and all of his crew disappeared without a trace during their second voyage in 1498.

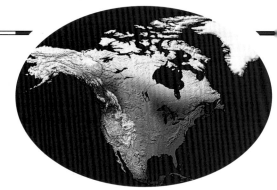

THE NORTHWEST PASSAGE

Once it was realized that this land above was not Asia but a new continent, explorers wanted to find a way around it. Ferdinand Magellan found a way around the southern tip of South America, so the French and English looked for a route through northern waters.

SIR MARTIN FROBISHER
-A Timeline-

~1576~
Sir Martin Frobisher looks for the Northwest Passage.

~1577~
Frobisher begins his second voyage in search of gold.

~1578~
Frobisher makes a second voyage to find the Northwest Passage.

Frobisher starts his third and last voyage in the quest for gold.

~1594~
Frobisher dies.

THE INUIT

The natives that Frobisher met in Canada called themselves Inuit. This translates in English as "people." Those who lived south of the Inuit called themselves Eskimo, which means "eaters of raw meat." Frobisher regarded them as savages, but they had devised a way of living in one of the harshest places known.

SAILING INTO DANGER

Explorers searching for the Northwest Passage soon discovered the dangers of such a voyage. The farther north they went, the colder the climate became. Ropes and sails would freeze, and there was the constant danger of icebergs and being stuck fast in an ice sheet.

FIGHTING THE INUIT

Frobisher's crew fought with the Inuit who had kidnapped five of his crew. He decided to capture an Inuit in a kayak. He drew the Inuit to his ship by ringing a bell over the side and then suddenly grabbing him. On his return to England, both the unfortunate Inuit and his kayak were presented to the king.

Voyages to North America

One of the reasons why Ferdinand and Isabella were not eager to allow Christopher Columbus to remain as governor of the newly discovered lands was due to the threat from other European powers, especially France and England. The Spanish believed that the French and English would try to claim the land for themselves, so they sent ships and weapons and set up colonies with powerful governors. It worked *too* well. The French and English explorers simply ignored the parts of South America that the Spanish had conquered. It would have been too costly in terms of money and lives to attempt to overthrow them. Instead, they turned their attention to the unexplored lands of North America and Canada.

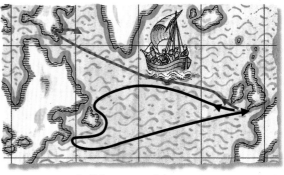

Frobisher ——— Cabot ———

SIR MARTIN FROBISHER

This picture shows Sir Martin Frobisher's crew fighting with the Inuit in Canada. Frobisher had sailed to Canada to try to discover the Northwest Passage to Asia. He set off from London in June 1576 with three ships. One ship sank off Greenland and another turned back after the crew mutinied. Frobisher sailed on and reached Baffin Island. He, too, thought, mistakenly, that he had found the route to Asia.

Rivalry for Empire

W hen James Cook was born, the parts of the world conquered by European powers were still thought to belong to them. Empires provided precious metals such as gold and silver, as well as timber and animal skins that could be used in trade. Spain thought the Pacific Ocean was part of her empire, which spread from the Philippine islands in the west to Central and South America in the east. However, during wars against France and Spain, the British navy began to penetrate the Pacific, undermining the idea that it was a "Spanish lake." In 1740–1744, Admiral George Anson attacked Spanish shipping off California before returning home via China. British forces also started attacking Spanish bases, such as Porto Bello, on the mainland of Central America.

COMMODORE GEORGE ANSON
(1697–1762)

In 1739, Great Britain and Spain began the War of Jenkins' Ear (so called because a British merchant ship captain claimed that a Spanish officer had cut off his ear), and Anson took a squadron of five British naval vessels into the Pacific to attack Spanish shipping and settlements. He returned home around the world with plunder worth $600,000 but lost 1,051 of his 1,955 men, mostly from scurvy and disease. On his return Anson was hailed as a hero and promoted to Rear Admiral.

A COMMEMORATIVE PLATE

Admiral Edward Vernon's capture of the Spanish town of Porto Bello was celebrated in England, and many commemorative items were produced for sale. This plate, made in London or Liverpool in 1740, depicts the Iron Castle under bombardment, with the town beyond.

RIVALRY FOR EMPIRE
-A TIMELINE-

~1509~
The Arab fleet is destroyed by the Portuguese at the Battle of Diu, marking the beginning of Portuguese trade domination in the Indian Ocean.

~1569~
Spain fights a war with Portugal over the Philippines and emerges victorious.

~1726~
Montevideo, Uruguay, is founded by the Spanish to prevent Portuguese expansion.

~1739~
The War of Jenkins' ear occurs.

The British capture the town of Porto Bello, Panama, from the Spanish.

MODEL OF A CHINESE GARDEN

After crossing the Pacific, Anson anchored in the Pearl River (Zhu Jiang), China, in 1744 to repair his ship. His attitude was too aggressive for the Chinese, and his presence disturbed merchants trying to maintain trade. However, he was given this model Chinese garden, the contents of which signify long life and include a peach tree in coral, a pine tree in carved wood and ivory, bamboos in tinted ivory, and rocks in malachite and rose quartz.

THE TAKING OF THE *NUESTRA SEÑORA DE COVADONGA*

While in the Pacific, Anson captured one of the Spanish treasure ships sailing from Acapulco, Mexico, to Manila, Philippines, with 1,313,843 pieces of eight and 2,231 lbs. (1,012kg) of silver onboard. Worth at least $600,000 then, it would be worth many millions today.

SWORD SURRENDERED IN PORTO BELLO

This sword, with its Parisian hilt and Spanish blade, was surrendered by the Spanish commandant of the Iron Castle in 1739.

THE CAPTURE OF PORTO BELLO

In 1739, a British squadron under Admiral Edward Vernon took the Spanish coastal town of Porto Bello in Panama, Central America. The town was defended by three castles, the first of which, Iron Castle, was bombarded into submission.

New Colonies

The idea of establishing new colonies around the world came slowly to the Elizabethans. The original motivation for exploring new countries arose first out of trade and the need to establish new markets and later from greed.

Even the Spaniards, who actually invaded parts of Central and South America, had little thought of colonization at first. What they craved was gold. England, the Netherlands, and France were quick to follow and readily plundered the Spanish ships returning home for their share of the booty. It would be another 200 years before England made any serious attempts at building an empire. When this did happen, it followed the same pattern of establishing colonies around trading posts, with the result that the British Empire was scattered across the globe along trade routes rather than radiating out from a coherent center.

VIRGINIA

England's first efforts at establishing colonies in North America failed, though they paved the way for later attempts and laid the foundations of what one day would become the British Empire. Sir Walter Raleigh established a small colony in Roanoke Island (now part of North Carolina) in 1584–1585 and christened the territory *Virginia* in honor of Elizabeth, the "virgin queen." Conditions proved too harsh, and the colonists met with hostile reactions from the local Native Americans, resulting in the colony being deserted by 1590.

CONQUISTADORS

At the time of the first European colonization of Central and South America, there were two dominant civilizations there: the Aztecs, centered in what is now Mexico, and the Inca of Peru and surrounding areas. Although technologically advanced, both societies were based on conquest and empire building rather than colonization and demanded tribute from those they defeated. Their societies emphasized domination, principally by high taxation to pay for monumental works, and their religions demanded sacrificial victims. When the Spanish conquered their lands in the 1500s, many of the ordinary people are said to have initially welcomed them as liberators rather than conquerors (conquistadors).

FAILED COLONY

Following the failure of Raleigh's colony in Roanoke Island, no further attempts at colonization were made by the Elizabethans. The colony of Virginia was eventually reestablished farther north and named Jamestown after King James I. This settlement was more successful, based on a thriving tobacco trade with England.

SAVED BY A PRINCESS

One of the early Virginian colonists, Captain John Smith befriended a Native American princess, Pocahontas. Her father was Powhatan, said to be the king of all the native tribes in the area, who remained suspicious of the English. Powhatan decided to slay all the white colonists and return the land to Indian rule, but Pocahontas risked her life to warn Smith and so avoided a massacre.

POCAHONTAS

Although Pocahontas saved the life of John Smith, he was hurt in the struggle and was sent home to England. She later married another prominent colonist, John Rolfe, and returned to England with him, where she was received at King James I's court. Pocahontas persuaded Rolfe to let her return to North America, but tragically, she died at the age of 22 on the eve of her departure (May 2, 1617) from either smallpox or a common cold and is buried in Gravesend, England.

NATIVE'S REVENGE

The Spanish conquerors of Central and South America defeated the local population within the space of only two years. Unfortunately, before any real attempts at colonization had been contemplated, the Spanish thirst for gold (which was in plentiful supply and was regarded by the natives as only of decorative value) reached almost fever pitch. The conquerors openly pillaged the land, especially in Mexico and Peru, in their search for riches. Although welcomed initially by the natives as saviors from a harsh military regime, the Spaniards soon took advantage and exploited them, killing and torturing thousands. Then they enslaved thousands more in the silver mines that they had discovered. The natives are seen here extracting their revenge by pouring molten gold down the throat of a captured conquistador.

THE SPANISH INVASION

One of the reasons for the speed with which Spain overtook the Aztec and Inca empires is that many conquered native tribes, hostile to their old enemies, actively aided the Spanish soldiers. Another reason was the Spanish use of guns, which were unheard of in South America. Cortés conquered the Aztec civilization in 1519–1520, completely destroying their capital of Tenochtitlán in the process, and built his own capital, Mexico City, on its ruins.

New Trade Routes

The need to discover new trade routes during Queen Elizabeth I's reign grew directly out of England's ongoing war with Spain. Spain was then the richest and most powerful country in Europe and had already extended her empire to most of the West Indies and Central America, jealously guarding the southern and western seaways. International trade was as important to the Elizabethan economy and society as it is today, and it became essential to open up new trade routes. Even though traveling by sea was hazardous, it was still preferable to overland transportation, which was hindered by poor roads and hostile countries. Sir Francis Drake and engaging in other Elizabethan seafarers began by simply stealing Spanish treasures and other blatant acts of piracy, but soon the need to establish new and longer-term trade routes became the priority.

SLAVE TRADE

The Spanish occupation of the Caribbean and South America had been ruthless, and many natives were slain. Many of the survivors proved unsuitable or unwilling to be employed as laborers, so there was a ready market for slaves exported from West Africa. The Spaniards strictly controlled the import of slaves into the colonies, but English mariners, including Drake and Hawkins, engaged in illicit slave trading to the Spanish Main and afterward to the new colonies of North America.

A SWEET TOOTH

Sugar had been available in England prior to the 1500s in the form of sugar beets (a root vegetable), but extraction was laborious. Sugar cane yielded a much more productive crop, but it would not grow in the English climate. Many sugar plantations were established in the West Indies, usually employing slave labor.

SOUTH CHINA SEA

Opening up new trade routes was not without its problems. From the mid-1500s on, trade between the Far East and Europe increased dramatically, so much so that heavily laden merchant ships soon became prime targets for pirate attacks. The South China Sea, between China, Japan, and the East Indies, was especially treacherous. Sometimes fleets of pirate vessels descended upon merchant ships. Favorite vessels of Chinese pirates were captured trading junks, as shown here, converted to carry guns. Eventually, influential merchant companies (such as the East India Company), who financed the voyages, persuaded the British government to protect merchant shipping.

RUSSIA

In 1553, Sir Hugh Willoughby and Richard Chancellor set out to discover the Northeast Passage. They became separated and Willoughby perished in the ice, but Chancellor went on to reach the Russian coast and then traveled overland to Moscow (shown above) the following year. He set up trade relations (principally in furs) between Russia and England but died off the coast of Scotland on a return trip in 1555.

UNUSUAL FOODS

Many of the foods brought back by Elizabethan seafarers were regarded as no more than interesting curiosities, such as the tomato (bottom right). Others, like the potato, quickly became firm favorites to supplement the often limited diet at the time. They were usually quite expensive, however, and were regarded as a delicacy until botanists succeeded in introducing the plants to the English climate. The introduction of culinary spices brought back from overseas was welcomed. Peppers and chilies, from South America (left), were used to disguise the often rancid taste of Elizabethan foods, while from the East Indies came spices such as cloves. During Drake's circumnavigation, he had to take onboard many unusual and exotic foods in order to sustain his crews. Among these was the coconut palm, which natives used as a major source of food, making oil from the kernels. Drake brought a coconut back to England, which he presented to Elizabeth as a memento of his voyage. The tobacco plant (above right) came from North America, where the Native Americans smoked it in clay pipes. Originally it was used as a medicine to purge the body of phlegm.

New Trade Routes

SIR THOMAS GRESHAM
(c. 1519–1579)

The cost of overseas voyages was very high and could not have been undertaken without financial backing from rich merchants. One of the foremost was Sir Thomas Gresham, who built the Royal Exchange in London.

Elizabethan expeditions reached destinations as far apart as Russia, North America, and Canada in the north and South America, Africa, and Asia in the south, looking for new trade routes. Their achievements were all the more incredible because of the length of time taken to complete the voyages in small vessels, often crossing uncharted seas. The importance of opening up new trade routes to Asia and the East Indies was paramount in the eyes of the Elizabethan merchant adventurers. Spices were the most prized and valuable commodities, achieving astronomical prices on the European markets.

The view shown here is of the tropical coast of Ceylon, now Sri Lanka, off the southeast coast of India.

THE BEGINNINGS OF EMPIRE

India and Ceylon had been known to European explorers since at least the time of Marco Polo (c. 1295) and would have been familiar to the Elizabethan seafarers on their frequent visits to the Spice Islands (the Moluccas). As elsewhere, the Elizabethans' prime concern was setting up new trade routes, but they frequently encountered strange new cultures, from primitive witch doctors in North America (see left) to the highly sophisticated and ancient cultures of Asia. In 1601, the East India Company received its royal charter, marking the beginning of Great Britain's first claims to an empire.

EUROPEAN DISEASES

One of the main reasons for the terrible drop in population was the introduction of diseases such as smallpox and measles into the South American continent. The peoples of South and Central America had no resistance to these new diseases, and many died as a result.

BECOMING EUROPEAN

The Spanish and Portuguese conquerors felt that their way of life and religion were better than those of the peoples they had conquered. This picture shows that people were forced out of their native clothes and made to wear European fashions. It was hoped this would make them more European.

SURVIVING CUSTOMS

The Europeans did not succeed in completely destroying the cultures they came across. This mask shows that modern Mexicans still celebrate the Day of the Dead, which has its origins with the Aztecs. Even today, many people in South and Central America add parts of their old religions to Christian worship.

DESTROYING IDOLS

The priests who traveled with the explorers were determined that the conquered peoples would become Christian. Many of these peoples felt that they had been defeated by a superior god and converted readily. The priests also stamped out all signs of the old religions by tearing down temples and smashing statues of gods. They replaced them with crosses and statues of the Virgin Mary.

Life in Spanish America

The arrival of the Spanish and Portuguese in South and Central America had a devastating effect on the peoples who were living there. In only a few years, huge empires were destroyed by small groups of determined and cruel men driven by greed, personal ambition, and religious zeal. These new rulers did not respect the ideas and customs of their new subjects. All over the conquered empires, the Spaniards and Portuguese looted and destroyed. The population of Mexico was estimated to be 25 million in 1519. From disease and murder, that figure had plummeted to almost two million by 1580.

INDEPENDENCE

It was only in the first part of the 1800s that South and Central America finally broke away from their European rulers. It was the revolutionary Simón Bolívar who led many countries toward independence. Paraguay became independent in 1813, followed by Argentina in 1816. Chile came next in 1818 and then Mexico and Peru in 1821.

NEW BUILDINGS

Once the Spaniards had destroyed the temples and buildings they came across, they began to build on top of the ruins. Churches, such as this one in Cuzco, were built on the sites of old temples. Mexico City was built on the remains of Tenochtitlán using stones from the dismantled buildings.

HARSH PUNISHMENTS

As more and more people from Spain voyaged to Mexico and South America, conditions for the conquered peoples continued to get worse. Thousands were enslaved and made to work in gold and silver mines, where they suffered from terrible conditions and overwork. This meant that their fields were left untended, and many more went hungry. Anyone who disobeyed the Spanish was severely dealt with. This picture shows people being burned alive by their Spanish master.

The Impact of South America on Europe

From the ruined palaces of ancient empires to the magnificent churches built by the Spanish and Portuguese, it is clear even today that the arrival of Europeans on American shores had a huge and devastating impact. Although it is more difficult to see the influence that South and Central America had on the lives of Europeans, they nevertheless had a similar impact. The most obvious result was the huge amount of gold and silver that was taken to Spain. The Spanish king claimed one fifth of all gold and silver that was mined. This made Spain one of the most powerful and wealthiest nations in Europe. It is still possible to see Spanish churches decorated with gold that came from their conquered lands. Most of the foods that we all take for granted were first grown in these lands.

NUTS AND BEANS

Many vegetables, such as peanuts, sweet potatoes, and kidney beans, came originally from South and Central America. They are now grown all over the world. Peanuts (above) are native to South America. They were first introduced to Africa by European explorers and then reached North America with the slave trade.

They are now cultivated all over the world, from India to Nigeria and the United States.

Sweet potatoes are native to Central America and were an important part of the Aztec diet and were also found in the Andes Mountains. They were taken to Europe in the 1500s and then later spread to Asia.

SQUASHES

Squashes such as pumpkins and zucchini were central to the diets of people in Central America. There is some evidence that they were eaten in North America before the 1400s. However, it was the arrival of the Spanish explorers that speeded up the spread of squashes. They are now grown and eaten all over the world, especially in Mediterranean countries and North America.

RUBBER AND MAHOGANY

Rubber was used by the peoples of South America for centuries. Christopher Columbus observed the inhabitants of Haiti using rubber to make balls for games. The Aztecs used rubber balls to play tlachtli. But it was not until the start of the 1800s, when a way was found to keep rubber soft when it became solid, that it began to be used commercially. Mahogany has been used for making fine furniture since 1500. European demand for mahogany led to many South American forests being cleared. Their continued destruction is a major concern for modern environmentalists.

GOODS FROM THE NEW WORLD
-A TIMELINE-

~1493~
Christopher Columbus introduces corn, sweet potatoes, and other goods from the New World to the Spanish court.

~1565~
Tobacco is first introduced to England.

~c. 1570~
The potato is introduced to Spain.

~1597~
Sir Walter Raleigh brings mahogany back from the West Indies to England.

CORN

Along with the sweet potato, corn was the most important crop of both South and Central America. The Aztecs ground corn into flour that was then turned into tortillas or tamales, which were stuffed with vegetables or atole, a type of porridge. The Inca also used corn to make a porridge called capia. The United States now grows almost one half of all the world's corn.

DID YOU KNOW?

Where did the design of ships like the *Endeavour* come from? The "cat-built" ships constructed for the coal trade on the northeast coast of England in James Cook's day were based on types captured from the Dutch in the Anglo-Dutch wars of 1652–1674. Because of their shallow waters and the need to load and unload vessels sitting on the foreshore, and because the Dutch grew rich from carrying bulky cargoes around the world, they designed very strong, flat-bottomed, roomy ships that proved ideal as a pattern for later English colliers.

What ships did the Europeans use as trading vessels? In the first part of the 1500s, the carrack became the most popular European ship for trade, exploration, and warfare. Carracks became important symbols of national pride. In England, King Henry VIII built the *Great Harry*, which was the largest carrack built up until that time. The French responded by building *La Grande Françoise,* which was even larger. Sadly, it was so large that it could not get out of the mouth of the harbor where it was built. By the end of the 1500s, the carrack was replaced by the galleon.

Who made up a ship's crew? Most ships not only had ordinary sailors among the crew but also carpenters, priests, cooks, doctors, gunners, blacksmiths, pilots, and boys as young as ten onboard. Crew members normally came from many different countries, and the captain sometimes had difficulty making them understand his instructions.

What was the biggest problem faced by sailors? The main problem faced by sailors on long voyages was scurvy. This often fatal disease is caused by a lack of vitamin C (ascorbic acid), which comes from fresh fruit and vegetables. Fresh food did not last long on the ships of the explorers. Sailors would become extremely tired and would start to bleed from the scalp and gums. However, it was not until 1915 that vitamins were identified. Citrus fruit juice was adopted against scurvy by the British Admiralty in 1795, but before that, fresh air, dry clothing, warmth, and exercise were also thought to help prevent it. There was thus a lot of confusion about its exact cause.

Where does the term "square meal" come from? It is not known when this term first came into use, but since at least Tudor times, meals onboard a ship were dished up on square platters, which seamen balanced on their laps. They had frames around the edges to prevent the food from falling off and were so shaped to enable them to be easily stored when not in use. Each sailor thus received his full ration, or square meal, for the day.

How does time give longitude? Every day (24 hours), Earth turns 360° from west to east; that is, it turns 15° of longitude every hour and 1° every four minutes. A place that has a four-minute difference in time at noon from a starting point (or prime meridian) to east or west—noon in each spot being when the Sun is exactly overhead—is 1° of longitude away. Thus, accurate east/west time variations between places can be converted into relative distances and positions of longitude.

Do we still use the stars to navigate? It is easy to assume that because navigational techniques used in the past were relatively simple that they were also inaccurate. This is not necessarily true, although results need to be accurately recorded and verified in order to be usable. In 1967, astronomers discovered pulsars, rapidly rotating condensed stars (formed from dead stars) that emit radio waves, or pulses, as detectable beams. They pulsate at fixed rates, making it possible for future space programs to utilize them for navigational purposes in outer space.

Where is Columbus buried? Columbus died on May 20, 1506 at his home in Valladolid in Spain. In 1513, his body was moved to a monastery in Seville. In 1542, Columbus's remains crossed the Atlantic Ocean to Hispaniola, and he was buried in the cathedral of Santa Maria in Santo Domingo, Dominican Republic. However, it is also claimed that Columbus's body lies in Havana, Cuba, or the cathedral of Seville, Spain.

How did the Spice Islands get their name? One of the main attractions for the Elizabethan explorers searching for new trade routes were spices from the East. The groups of islands that make up the East Indies (which include the Moluccas, Philippines, and Melanesia groups of islands) were especially rich in such commodities, and they came to be collectively known as the Spice Islands.

What happened to Drake's Drum? During World War II, stories circulated of warships supposedly carrying Drake's Drum that were miraculously saved from disaster after the ghostly sounds of drumming were heard. In truth, the drum has never been carried onboard any ship since its return to England in the 1500s, and during World War II, it was locked away for safekeeping. Replicas may have been carried onboard ships, but not the original, which is displayed is displayed at Buckland Abbey in Devon.

How did *America* get its name? North and South America was named after the 16th-century navigator and mapmaker Amerigo Vespucci. Of Italian birth, in 1508, he was named Chief Royal Pilot of Spain. All Spanish captains had to provide him with full details each time they undertook a new voyage so that he could constantly amend and update his collection of sea charts. He made several voyages to the New World himself (notably in 1499–1500) and was once credited with discovering the Americas. Although this was not true, he was the first person to consider them to be independent continents and not part of Asia. They were afterward known as "Amerigo's Land" in honor of him.

How did Islam spread within Africa? In Africa, most peoples followed their own religions and customs. However, the part of Africa that lay around the Sahara Desert was dominated by Islam. It was introduced into Africa from two directions. Just south of the Sahara is an area known as the Sahel. For centuries, people in the Sahel crossed the Sahara to trade with the Mediterranean. When Islam spread across North Africa in the 600s and 700s, Islam found its way across the desert with the traders. On the East African coast, Islam arrived with Arab merchants who sailed down most of the East African coastline.

Where is Cook buried? The Hawaiians partly ate and then burned Cook's body, according to custom. A few days later, when relations with his men had improved, they returned most of his bones. On February 21, 1779, his remains were buried at sea in a full naval ceremony, just offshore of Kealakekua Bay, where he was killed. A monument there marks the site of his death.

How much were the European explorers involved in slavery? From the 1440s, the Portuguese used their expeditions along the West African coast to capture people and take them back to Portugal to sell as slaves. Europeans felt that slavery was justified because the people they had captured were not Christians. Once they became slaves, they could become Christians. Africans began to fight back once they realized why the Europeans were there. Portuguese traders soon realized that it would be easier to buy slaves from traders in Benin.

How did the Portuguese discover Brazil? When Vasco da Gama returned to Portugal from the Indies, Pedro Álvares Cabral set off from Lisbon with a fleet of 13 ships in March 1500. Like da Gama, he began by sailing westward. However, he went much farther than he intended. On April 22, he sighted the coast of Brazil. After claiming the land for Portugal, he set off eastward for the Indies.

What is the history of the ancient civilizations before the explorers "discovered" them? We know very little about the lives of the Aztecs and Inca because the Spaniards destroyed everything they found. Beautiful gold objects were melted down into gold bars. Books and drawings were burned as works of the devil. Bishop Diego de Landa Calderón of the Yucatán came across some painted books, and later he wrote: "We found a great number of books in these letters of theirs, and because they had nothing but superstition and lies of the devil, we burned them all, which greatly upset the Indians and caused them much pain." Most of the remains of Tenochtitlán were not discovered until the Mexicans began to build a subway in Mexico City.

How did the Aztec calendar work? The Aztec calendar stone worked in a very peculiar way. The calendar was made up of two wheels, one on top of the other. The small wheel had 13 numbers carved or painted on it. The large wheel had the names of 20 days on it; these were the names of animals or plants. Numbers could then be lined up with a particular named day. Only the Aztec priests could read these and tell if a day was to be lucky or unlucky. For instance, "4 Dog" was a good day to be born on. Anybody born on "2 Rabbit" would not fare so well. "1 Ocelot" was seen as a good day for traveling.

Which continent is the coldest, driest, highest, and windiest? Antarctica covers an area half as large as the U.S. (around 5.4 million sq. mi./14 million square km) and represents one tenth of Earth's landmass. Approximately 98 percent of Antarctica is covered by ice, up to 1.5 mi. (2.4km) thick in places. The Elizabethan explorers had searched in vain for a habitable landmass in the southern oceans, which was discovered in 1820 when Edward Bransfield landed on part of the Antarctic peninsula.

GLOSSARY

amber Fossil tree resin, *(see below)* that is usually orange-brown in color. Amber is often used in jewelry.

amputation The surgical removal of a limb or body part.

anesthetic A drug that causes temporary loss of sensation in the body.

armada A large fleet of warships.

astronomical Relating to the study of the universe beyond Earth.

awning A canopylike covering attached to the exterior of a building to provide shelter.

baptism A Christian ceremony that signifies spiritual cleansing and rebirth.

bombardment The heavy continuous attacking of a target with artillery.

botany The scientific study of plants and vegetation.

cannibal A person who eats the flesh of other humans.

"cat boat" A large vessel often used in the coal trade. The origins of the name are a mystery, but one theory is that the name comes from **c**oal **a**nd **t**imber—which these boats often transported.

charter To lease or rent services and possessions; a document issued by an authority that grants an institution certain rights or privileges.

charting Navigational mapping of coastlines and seas so that sailors can find routes for purposes of trade and exploration.

circumnavigate To travel all the way around something.

civil war A war between different groups in the same country.

colonization The extension of a nation's power by the establishment of settlements and trade in foreign lands.

commission A committee set up to deal with and look at a certain issue.

dead reckoning A method of estimating one's current position based on a known previous position, allowing for speed, distance, and direction moved.

deck A platform built on a ship. There are often numerous decks on a ship.

dissolution The process of breaking up and destroying something. The Dissolution of the Monasteries was a process undertaken by England's King Henry VIII between 1536 and 1540 that resulted in the disbanding of all monasteries, nunneries, and friaries and claiming of their income, wealth, and land for the king.

draft The depth to which a ship sinks in the water, measured from its keel.

dysentery An inflammatory infection of the intestines resulting in severe diarrhea. Dysentery was a major cause of death onboard a ship.

electrical charge Electrical energy that has been stored.

equator The imaginary line running across the center of Earth from east and west, at an equal distant from the North and South poles.

expulsion The act of forcing something or someone out.

Global Positioning System (GPS) A satellite system that allows users to pinpoint their location.

haberdasher A person who sells items for men's attire.

hawk bells Bells attached to the legs of a hawk by a small leather strap just above the talons. Bells were often organized to ring with different tones so that in a group of hawks, a pleasant sound would be produced. Hawking was a popular country sport where a hawk hunted for its owner.

hulk A ship that is afloat but that is not capable of going to sea. It often refers to a ship that has had its rigging or equipment removed.

interior The inland part of a country.

junk A Chinese sailing ship.

keel The structural main beam running down the middle of a ship, serving as the spine of the boat's structure.

kingdom A country with a king or queen at its head.

latitude The imaginary parallel lines running east to west around Earth.

longitude The imaginary parallel lines running north to south around Earth.

malaria A disease spread by the bite of a mosquito.

missionary A person who tries to convert native inhabitants to their own religious viewpoint. Missionaries often provide charitable services.

mortality The likelihood of death. The mortality rate is the rate of death in a certain number of people in a population.

musket A muzzleloading smoothbore gun (without rotational grooves to guide the projectile along the barrel) mounted in and fired from the shoulder.

mutiny A rebellion by members of a ship's crew to overthrow the captain.

native A person born in a particular place or country and who lives there.

observatory A building designed and equipped for looking at the stars and watching astronomical events.

pack ice A large collection of ice that has combined to form a single masss. Pack ice moves with the sea's currents.

patronage The support, encouragement, and backing (often financial) of a person or people.

piracy Stealing while at sea; taking ships and possessions without the instruction of a sovereign or ruler.

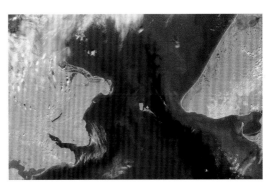

Aerial view of the Bering Strait. Russia is to the left and Alaska is to the right.

primitive Relating to an early stage of technical or technological progress; a person who belongs to an early stage of civilized advancement.

purser The person onboard a ship who is responsible for all things financial.

putrefaction The decomposition or breakdown of a dead creature.

pyramid A building or structure with triangular sides, narrowing to a peak at the top.

sheer legs A structure of two or three wooden beams tied together to form a support for lifting heavy weights.

Spanish Inquisition The Spanish Inquisition was set up in 1478 by Ferdinand and Isabella of Spain. Its purpose was to ensure that Catholic orthodoxy was maintained in Spain.

Spanish Main The mainland coast of the Spanish Empire around the Carribean.

strait A narrow sea channel joining two larger bodies of water.

subdue To put down or contain by force or authority.

sugar cane A tall, fibrous, grasslike plan that naturally contains high levels of sucrose, which is refined to produce sugar.

tribute The tax system employed by the Aztecs to support their state. This was paid by all the regions under their control to finance construction, military, nobility, and religion.

typhoid An illness caused by eating or drinking contaminated food or water.

zealous Filled with enthusiasm and energy in favor of a cause.

zenith The point directly above a certain location.

INDEX